OFF THE GARDEN PATH

GREEN WONDERS OF THE WORLD

DANIEL AUSTIN

Published by Beyond Green

ISBN: 978-0-6452284-0-3 (paperback)

First edition, 2021

Cover photo courtesy of Gardens by the Bay

For book orders and enquiries, contact:
Email: sales@beyond-green-australia.com.au

NATIONAL LIBRARY OF AUSTRALIA

A catalogue record for this book is available from the National Library of Australia

Contents

Preface

They say life is what happens to you while you are busy making other plans, and looking back on mine, the adage rings true. Through the culmination of unlikely twists of fortune and an interest in plants, my life spiralled into an unplanned botanical odyssey in the blink of an eye.

Off the Garden Path: Green Wonders of the World was initially conceived as a way to share some of the remarkable horticultural enterprises I have been fortunate enough to be involved with around the world in the hope of inspiring gardeners and travellers alike. However, it soon became a book for anyone with an interest in the wonders of our planet.

Countless texts have been written on great gardens of the world. The titles have interwoven subgenres of design, history, the environment, and many other topics, but few have strayed from convention. Drawing inspiration from the likes of naturalists, past and present, I wanted to produce something else. I wanted to create something that would explore the wonderful world of plants while taking readers to extraordinary places they may otherwise never get to visit – in some cases, places they may not want to visit.

It seemed like a logical combination and as the research into plants of these regions became more concentrated, the organisms began to reveal amazing evolutionary traits just as interesting as the sites being featured. What started as a celebration of ethnobotanical photography quickly evolved into a valuable horticultural resource, and it soon became clear I would not complete the book alone. Over the years since its conception, the project has become an international collaboration benefitting from the input of several organisations around the world and even more individuals.

Though the text itself has been written over only a few years, the content has been collected over a lifetime, and I sincerely hope you enjoy the journey ahead as much as I have enjoyed putting it together.

Judaean Desert, Israel

Acknowledgements

The list of people who should be acknowledged in helping this book come to fruition is a long one.

First and foremost, I would like to thank the horticulturists who have directly contributed to the work by sharing their knowledge, images, or research. This book would not exist without the valuable assistance of the following individuals:

Dr. Ori Fragman-Sapir, the Scientific Director of The Jerusalem Botanical Gardens in Israel, has a wealth of knowledge on plants of the Middle East. A sincere and dedicated botanist, his training and assistance in plant identification have contributed enormously to the book's value as a botanical reference.

Sofi Mursidiwati, Curator at the Bogor Centre for Conservation Research and Botanic Gardens in Indonesia has contributed several images to the book and shared her research into the enigmatic *Rafflesia* genus. I met Sofi when I wandered into parts of the Bogor Botanic Gardens that were out of bounds, and instead of chasing me out of the off-limits research area, she invited me in. It was an illustration of her genuine passion in the field, as is her contribution to this book.

Matt Coulter, the Senior Horticultural Curator at the Mount Lofty Botanic Gardens Nursery in South Australia, has contributed images and research findings to this project. He is considered a world authority in *Amorphophallus titanum* propagation and has honed the techniques over many years. The chapter discussing the conservation of the species would have been much shorter if not for Matt's contributions.

Anton Van Der Schans is the Principal Horticulturist at Singapore's Gardens by the Bay. He has provided personal insights and a wealth of knowledge about the extensive site. The Gardens by the Bay have also contributed some beautiful images to the book.

Many more friends and colleagues around the world have contributed in some shape or form, too numerous to list. Whether through the exchange of knowledge or just friendship while I passed through their parts of the world, I appreciate and thank them all.

Beyond horticulture, putting together this project involved navigating the world of literature and publishing. As a layman in the field, I must thank some more experienced mentors who provided valuable advice and encouragement during this project. Members of the Horticultural Media Association of Australia, Karen Smith and Trevor Nottle have been instrumental in this regard.

I'm also thankful to have crossed paths with Ines Parker early in the project. A member of the South Australian Mediterranean Garden Society and publication co-editor, Ines worked with me out of pure interest in the book for over a year, assisting with chapter edits and polishing the structure of the text. The book would not be the same without her input and many hours of contribution.

Lastly, I would like to thank my beautiful wife, Auria. I am sure the canals of Venice sound more romantic than floating farms in Myanmar, but she has been mad enough to accompany me on several of the trips used to create this work. An adventure is an adventure, and any chance to travel is a good one, but Auria has also put up with the times in between travelling for the book. Times when I have been stuck to the computer for days, only pulling away to recite edits of my latest chapter ad nauseum. The woman has the patience of a saint.

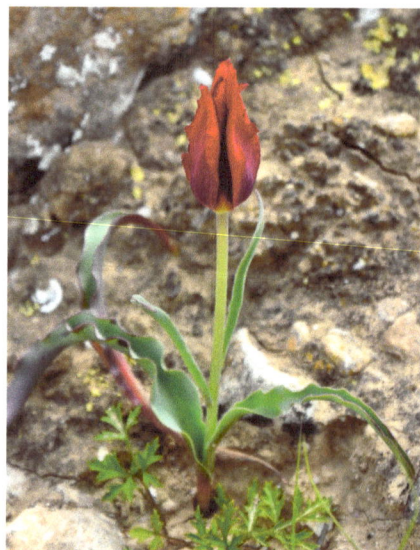

Wild tulip, *Tulipa systola*, Israel

Introduction

Plants have the power to build, change and enhance cultures. Over centuries they have influenced everything from religion and medicine to transport and construction. The world's flora has thrived, evolved, and endured for millions of years. These organisms have spread to occupy the farthest reaches of Earth and adapted to the most inhospitable of conditions in doing so.

How is it that these seemingly inanimate lifeforms have been so successful?

Far from the passive image we perceive, plants are engaging in a perpetual battle for survival, and the tactics they employ to gain an advantage are amazing. Some engage in chemical warfare; others mobilise armies. Many have even manipulated humans into ensuring their success. To gain a true appreciation of their world, it's time to take a deep breath, open your mind and step off the garden path.

While exploring some of the world's most wondrous horticultural enterprises in some of the most exotic locations our planet has to offer, the traditional definition of a garden is about to be tested, challenged, and transformed. Whether it is gaining an insight into the lives of subsistence farmers in rural Tanzania, drifting among the floating farms of Myanmar, or learning how researchers are preserving the world's largest flowers in Indonesia - the pages ahead will have you questioning what it really means to be a gardener.

A collection of the world's green wonders, these sights are an illustration of what occurs when extraordinary plants cross paths with remarkable people.

Gardens of the Taj Mahal, India

Custodians of a Flooded Forest
The Ratargul Forest
Sylhet, Bangladesh

Life with water in abundance

As one of the most populous nations on Earth, Bangladesh may not evoke visions of serene landscapes, but home to the world's largest and most fertile delta system, the Ganges Delta, lush floral diversity is displayed in abundance. The Sundarban mangroves of the country are perhaps the most extensive example and attract thousands of visitors annually. Known to provide critical habitat for numerous species, including the endangered Bengal tiger (*Panthera tigris tigris*), the immense mangrove system is one of the world's largest. Spreading over ten thousand square

Bengal tiger prowling the Sundarbans

kilometres, the site spans much of southern Bangladesh and extends into West Bengal in India. Named after the dominant Sundari mangrove (*Heritiera fomes)*, the Sundarbans blanket the Ganges Delta and fed by several river systems, are constantly inundated with water.

Mangrove-rich delta systems are true green wonders of the world. Important havens of biodiversity, they can be found across the planet where riverine networks meet oceans, but Bangladesh is also home to a rarer riparian wonder. Edging the country's northern border with India, a remarkable flooding forest that transforms with the seasons can be found. One of just a handful of these unique ecosystems globally, the Ratargul Forest exists in relative obscurity compared to its larger geographical cousin of the Ganges Delta but is just as spectacular.

Aerial view of the Ratargul Forest

Ratargul Forest in the dry season

Ratargul Forest is one of the very few climatic niches known as 'freshwater swamp forests' or, more appealingly, 'flooded forests', which occur worldwide. These unusual environments are characterised by landscapes that remain underwater for much of the year, but rather than maintaining consistent water levels, the forests undergo dramatic changes throughout the seasons. At times, portions of the forests may dry out completely, while during other periods, water levels may be so high the areas resemble lakes.

Bangladesh has a subtropical monsoonal climate characterised by three distinct seasons. A hot, humid summer is experienced from March to June; a rainy monsoon season takes effect from June to October; and a cool, dry winter persists from October to March. Sustained by rivers transporting monsoonal rains from as far away as India, the waters of the Ratargul Forest reach depths of nearly ten metres in the

The flooded forest at full saturation

CUSTODIANS OF A FLOODED FOREST

3

wettest seasons, and the region is only accessible by boat. In the drier winter, water persists only in the deeper depressions of the landscape, so much of the area is navigable on foot. Because of its rare environmental conditions, the location has been declared a 'Special Biosphere Reserve' by the government of Bangladesh - a valid title given the biodiversity present within the forest.

Woman weaving shitol pati

Surviving the floods

Like the Sundarbans in the south of Bangladesh, Ratargul Forest takes its title from a prevalent plant species in the area. Known locally as rata (*Schumannianthus dichotomus)*, the specimens are among several highly adaptable plants that contribute to the landscape and its ecology. Occurring throughout Southeast Asia, where it is known by many other names, rata is of particular importance in Bangladesh, both culturally and economically. Fibres derived from the stems of the plant are used for weaving a traditional form of mat used across the country. The mats known as 'shitol pati' (translated as cool mat) are naturally cool to the touch. It's a valuable quality in the tropics and has contributed to the creations becoming firmly ingrained in Bangladeshi culture.

The mats are used in a variety of ways, from bedding and prayer to decoration. Shitol pati are formed by dying and weaving strips of rata stems that have been boiled in a botanical concoction, including rice water and giant crepe myrtle (*Lagerstroemia speciosa*) to soften the material. One mat can take several weeks to produce, depending on its intricacy. Cultivated and occurring naturally in riparian areas across the country, rata is a vital income source for rural communities. It is central to the livelihoods of thousands of families in Bangladesh. The United Nations Educational, Scientific and Cultural Organisation (UNESCO)

Exposed roots revealing how much the water level has receded in the forest

has recognised the shitol pati mats as a part of the organisation's list of 'Intangible Cultural Heritage,' illustrating just how significant the quintessentially Bangladeshi product is.

S. dichotomus is only one of over seventy plant species that can be found in the Ratargul Forest, an impressive tally, given the area remains underwater for much of the year. In the wet season, only the tree species, larger shrubs, and occasional climbers are seen above the surface of the swampy waters. However, as the area dries out and water levels recede, the botanical pallet of the site increases. Exposed soil gives seeds a chance to germinate, and herbaceous species lying dormant again become active.

Karanja *(Millettia pinnata)*

A flooded forest is a harsh environment to endure physiologically. Aquatic plants struggle with periodic drying, and the landscape can face high temperatures in the muddy periods between the flooded wet seasons and the cooler dry periods. However, for traditional terrestrial species, it is the rising waters that present a threat. Plants sensitive to flooding rapidly lose the oxygen supply to their roots when inundated with moisture, reducing nearly all metabolic activities, including cell division and nutrient absorption. Eventually, this absence of oxygen leads to a condition known as anoxia and the plant's death. It's a cause of death shared with many overwatered houseplants around the world.

Salinity can also pose a threat to plants during periods of flooding. At saturation, plant cells are far more prone to dehydration or rupturing through osmotic processes in the presence of salts. However, the plants that persist throughout the year in the Ratargul Forest can withstand the hazards presented by both dry and saturated conditions. They are a highly adaptable group of plants known as flood-tolerant hydrophytes.

Specially adapted roots survive both dry and saturated conditions

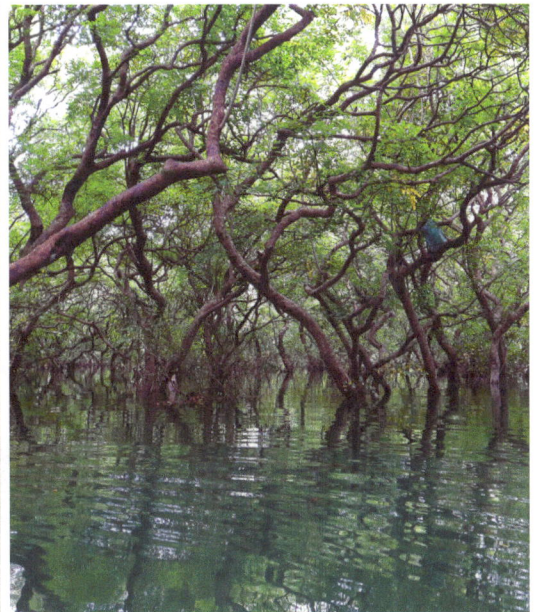
Ratargul Forest during the wet season

Blue water lily *(Nymphaea nouchali)*

Barun tree *(Crataeva magna)*

Sensitive plant *(Mimosa pudica)*

While the uptake of oxygen through plant roots facilitates important metabolic processes, plants also undertake gaseous exchange through their leaves and stems. Consequently, these organs become increasingly crucial for hydrophytic plants, which display a range of evolutionary adaptations to survive in the oxygen-deficient soils of flooded forests across the world.

The dominant tree species at the Ratargul Forest include freshwater mangroves (*Barringtonia acutangula*), figs (*Ficus religiosa* and *F. hispida*), karanja (*Millettia pinnata*), karoch (*Dalbergia reniformis*), and several others. The reason for the survival and prevalence of these species is revealed when water levels drop in the dry season and expose the otherworldly root systems of the trees, concealed for much of the year. Known as prop roots, these structures produce pores in their outer layers above any floodwaters' surface, which allow for oxygen intake and transport to lower submerged roots. Instead of prop roots, *F. religiosa* utilises roots, which swell and expand at the base of the trunk, increasing air space and providing extra support to prevent the trees from toppling over in the saturated soils.

Smaller shrubs and climbers without these root modifications also persist in the forest. Many initiate early and rapid shoot growth, which ensures that their stems make it above the water's surface quickly during flooding, so they can assist in acquiring oxygen. Some plants of the flooded forest have evolved 'aerenchyma'; these air spaces in the roots and stems of plants, allow diffusion of oxygen from the aerial portions of the plant into the roots. In most plants, the portion of plant tissues occupied by air is about five percent of their volume, while the tissues of wetland species can possess up to sixty percent pore space in some circumstances.

The porous stems of the blue water lily (*Nymphaea nouchali*) are a great example. The national flower of Bangladesh, *N. nouchali*, spends parts of its life dormant beneath boggy soils inundated with water. Then, when temperatures and water levels are ideal, the plants grow towards the water's surface, where they flower.

Their fleshy stems ensure the plants can metabolise adequate oxygen while being anchored to the waterlogged soil of the flooded forest floor.

N. nouchali has value medicinally, and like all water lilies, most parts of the plant are edible. The species is not alone in its medicinal and culinary value, and many of the plants of Ratargul follow this pattern. Karanja (*Millettia pinnata*) is a source of wood, insect repellent, and dye. The beautiful barun tree (*Crataeva magna)* is used in traditional Ayurvedic medicine, as are many of the trees, shrubs, and herbs growing with it. The local rose (*Rosa clinophylla*) is used for breeding commercial varieties because of its ability to withstand the demanding variations in the environment. In fact, it is hard to find a plant in the forest that is not useful.

Though valuable, not all the plants growing in Ratargul Forest are native. The conditions are ideal for exotic rattan (*Calamus guruba*), planted deliberately for its use in wicker products. Another alien species appearing with the many indigenous herbs sprouting in the dry season is particularly curious. The sensitive plant (*Mimosa pudica*) is both loved and hated around the world. It has naturalised in many countries and is a serious weed, but it has the remarkable ability to react to touch so dramatically, collectors still pursue it. Inarguably, it is hard not to be impressed as the plant's leaves appear to collapse and recoil at your fingertips.

The physiology responsible for the rapid movement in the leaves and stems of *M. pudica* has been researched and debated for many years and involves several steps. First, the stimulus of the contact is recognised by the plant; then, an electrical impulse drives the rapid release of a minute amount of moisture from specialised cells in the leaflets and leaf stems. This results in a loss of rigidity and the plants appearing to shy away from the contact. The novelty is actually the result of a complex biophysical reaction, but regardless of the chemistry involved, the movements of the sensitive plant have baffled and entertained for centuries.

Fish from the flooded forest are an important food source for the local population

Balance in a habitat that changes with the seasons

With a diverse collection of plants providing a solid foundation for the food chain and water in abundance, it is no wonder the fauna found in the Ratargul Forest is just as varied as the flora. Few animals persist throughout the year in the area, and permanent residence is restricted to insects, reptiles that can swim, amphibians, birds, and fish. More frequently, species will arrive when conditions are favourable and move on as the climate becomes adverse. At their wettest, the waters of Ratargul are home to over ninety species of fish arriving from adjoining rivers, but as the dry season takes hold, the number of fish species in the remaining wet areas reduces to around just ten. As waters drop, the muddy transition to the dry season provides perfect conditions for migratory birds to feed in the shallow waters, with around one hundred and seventy-five bird species seen throughout the year.

Man made fish farms are scattered throughout Ratargul

The arrival of the dry winter season is perhaps the most dramatic period at Ratargul Forest and sees an explosive migration of terrestrial fauna. Small animals, including rats, squirrels, macaques, and shrews, again have access to the area and soon provide a food source for larger predators, including mongoose, jungle cats, jackals, civets, and snakes. Even slow-moving porcupines meander in from the surrounding countryside to feed during this climatic window of abundance.

A changing world of increasing pressure

At over two hundred hectares, Ratargul Forest offers a productive environment that accommodates a vast collection of plants and animals. Unfortunately, this productivity leaves the area open to exploitation. The dry season that feeds so many terrestrial animals also offers enticing pasture for local shepherds and allowing livestock to graze on the plants in the delicate ecosystem is a temptation too great for some. The waters are an important fishery and sustain local communities, but with populations soaring in the surrounds of Ratargul, many species are increasingly overfished. There are laws in place to protect against illegal fishing, though they are inadequately policed. The same is true of illegal hunting and prohibited collection of timber at the site.

The drying forest becomes appealing habitat for land-based fauna

As the monsoon season ends and visitor numbers dwindle, boats are brought ashore throughout the swamp

One way to mitigate against some of these pressures has been to increase ecotourism in the area. The idea being, if local communities derive an income from visitors, it will demonstrate that protecting and maintaining the biodiversity of the forest could be as financially valuable as the quick monetary gains achieved through destructive practices. With an ideal location close to picturesque tea plantations, tourism has certainly been embraced at Ratargul. The forest is peppered with wooden boats and boatmen, paddles ready, to accommodate any arriving tourists. A local tradition of flute playing means that even the boatmen whose services have not been engaged will likely contribute to any visitor's experience, as they add to a magical forest soundtrack while waiting for customers of their own.

The delicate flora of the forest is at risk from farmers allowing livestock to graze in the area

Fish traps are largely unregulated

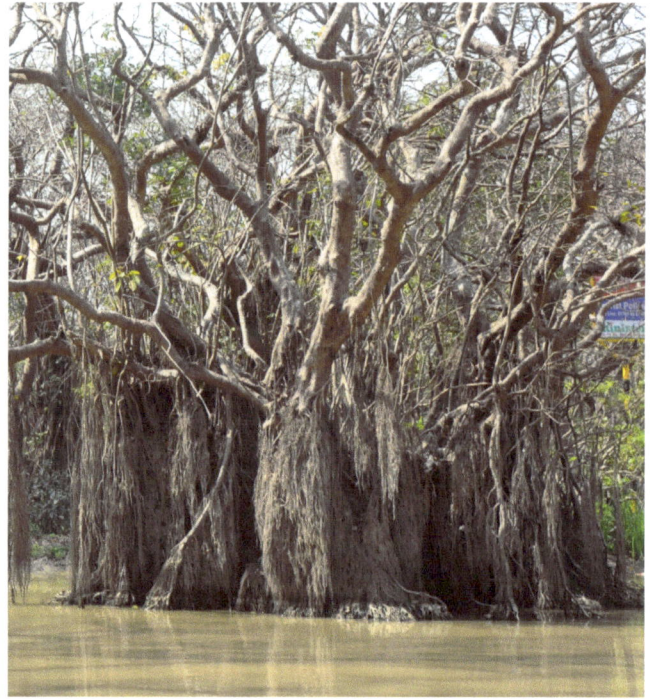
Otherworldly appearance of Ratargul in the dry season

Tourism should be a part of Ratargul's future, ensuring the area can be studied, explored, and appreciated for the marvel that it is, but the tourism industry presents its own problems. If left unregulated, the sheer numbers of tourists navigating the forest pose a threat to the delicate balance of the habitat and have the potential to influence animals' abilities to feed and breed normally. Thankfully the boats used to transport sightseers are engineless, and low impact, so minimal disturbance visitation is possible. Additionally, careless visitors often bring with them pollution and the scourge of plastics, which can have lasting implications in an environment like the Ratargul Forest.

Little known to the outside world and even within greater Bangladesh, the Ratargul Forest is approaching a critical time in its existence. There is an awareness of the delicacy of the ecosystem, a realisation that the area's governance has been lacking, and an acknowledgement of the diverse stakeholders, whose livelihoods depend on the flooded forest. While Ratargul is unique, this scenario is not, and around the world, in similar situations, a movement toward participatory forest management is

Tea plantation near the flooded forest

Central look out at the World Heritage site

OFF THE GARDEN PATH

returning increasingly positive results. Internationally, participatory forest management has been given various titles including, social forestry, adaptive co-management, and community-based natural resource management. In essence, it is a collaborative approach to managing natural resources that sees greater power and responsibility given to the people in regions where the resources exist.

Local man walking in the forest during the dry season

As a result of ongoing education programs, the people that rely on the Ratargul Forest are taking ownership of the area and its challenges. Sometimes terrestrial woodland, other times an aquatic swamp, and often falling somewhere in between, the ecosystem within the flooded forest has always existed in a precarious balance. However, in recent years, the local community is realising they are part of the equation deciding just how the scales might tip for Ratargul. Unfortunately, this does not solve the difficulties surrounding the conservation of the unique ecosystem. Creating awareness within the population is just the beginning of a long and challenging journey - but it is a beginning.

Across the planet, riparian ecosystems are renowned for fostering biodiversity. Whether areas are periodically flooded or endure constant moisture, flora and fauna encountered in these regions often blur the lines between the aquatic and terrestrial. Freshwater flooded forests are among the most remarkable examples and veiled in the monsoonal rains of the far northern reaches of Bangladesh; the Ratargul Forest is a perfect illustration of why they are so special.

The guardians of this forest are not your average gardeners, and Ratargul is not an average garden, but the custodians tasked with the care of this special place are aiming for the same holy trinity of horticulture pursued by gardeners the world over – achieving greenspace that is healthy, productive and aesthetically pleasing.

Mother and daughter navigating the forest in an engineless canoe

Greening the Desert
Farming in ultimate desolation
Aquba and Jabal Al-Madbah, Jordan

Insights into a cradle of civilisation

Bordered by Saudi Arabia, Iraq, Syria, Israel, and Palestine lies a country of such unique scenery; its landscapes are pursued generation after generation to feature as the backdrops in the classics of the silver screen. The Hashemite Kingdom of Jordan is an oasis in the sometimes-turbulent Levant region of the Middle East, and displaying relative stability for decades, Jordan is now an increasingly popular hotspot for international travellers. From diving with the teeming marine life and war-torn wrecks of the Red Sea to exploring the dreamy desolation of the Wadi Rum Valley, when it comes to once-in-a-lifetime experiences, Jordan delivers in spades.

Although the country hosts a diverse range of ecosystems and environments within its varied landscapes, Jordan is among the world's least forested nations. In many parts of the country, it would be reasonable to assume the inhospitable terrain might be far too harsh to foster any plant growth and to question if a garden by any definition would even be possible. Still, like plants themselves, gardeners here are surprisingly adaptable.

Regarded as a 'cradle of civilisation' from which some of the earliest human societies emerged, the fertile crescent is a region in the Middle East that curves from the Persian Gulf through modern-day Iraq, Syria, Lebanon, Jordan, Israel, and northern Egypt. As a result of its location, Jordan displays historical architecture that provides an opportunity for visitors to be transported back in time, to walk among the ruins of forgotten societies of the past.

The land, which is now known as Jordan, has formed part of numerous empires over the ages. However, it was the ancient Arabian nomads of the Nabatean Kingdom flourishing in the region between the fourth century BCE and first century CE who were responsible for constructing Jordan's most iconic early cities. Of these, there is none more impressive than the ancient Nabatean capital of Petra.

Wadi Rum at sunset

The remains of a carved camel and trader at Petra

Concealed in time and shifting sands for hundreds of years, the crumbling stone city of Petra tells the tale of a lost civilisation. Visiting the once expansive centre, etched into the desert mountains of southwest Jordan, is a truly surreal experience. Arrival to the city is by a sandy foot track at the base of a narrow stone gorge known as the Siq. Seventy metres tall at times and so constricted in parts that the stone obstructs the light from the sun above, it is clear this entrance was methodically planned. It offered no chance to flee should the city's Nabatean rulers have launched any sort of attack all those years ago.

Carved into the canyon walls stand the weathered remnants of camels forming part of a grand caravan which would have been awe-inspiring to any weary traveller visiting the city at its peak more than two thousand years ago. The caravan carving hints that the gloomy passage is coming to an end and soon after, Petra is announced in spectacular architectural drama with the appearance of the city's most famous landmark - the Treasury.

At over forty metres in height, the Treasury's original purpose is still debated along with many of the structures found throughout the ruins of the enormous city, which spanned well over two hundred and fifty square kilometres. To visit Petra today is to witness a harsh and crumbling landscape of scant greenery. However, with some observation, it quickly becomes apparent that there are many plant species perfectly adapted to the environment

The Treasury at Petra

Petra was a large and extensive city

and thriving. Native Mediterranean cypress (*Cupressus sempervirens*) and Phoenician juniper (*Juniperus phoenicea*) are among the sparse tree species surviving on the area's natural rainfall.

C. sempervirens has long been prized across the Mediterranean for its ability to thrive in hot, dry summers and its durable, scented wood. Timber cut centuries ago can still be found in excellent condition, from the ancient doors of St Peter's Basilica in the Vatican City to an array of antique musical instruments seen across the region. The longevity of the timber is impressive, as is the species' lifespan, with some specimens in Iran thought to be close to four thousand years old.

Native conifers and carved stone dwelling

Mysterious masters of the desert climate

While there are many healthy tree specimens to be found, the precipitation at Petra is unpredictable. The winding mountain trails connecting the ancient city also reveal the skeletal remains of trees that have fallen victim to extended dry periods. Water is a scarce commodity for the naturally occurring flora, and plants are most visible in lower gullies, where the precious substance may collect when rainfall is received. Even small fissures in the stone cliffs offer a minute increase in moisture compared to their exposed surroundings. They are ideal for the seeds of adaptable species, including the Persian pistachio (*Pistacia khinjuk*) to germinate and attempt survival in the near epiphytic conditions.

As trees are sparse in this part of the world, species like *P. khinjuk* have been well researched over the years and utilised for everything from timber and valuable resins to tanning agents in leather preparation. The valuable species also produce seeds that are edible when roasted.

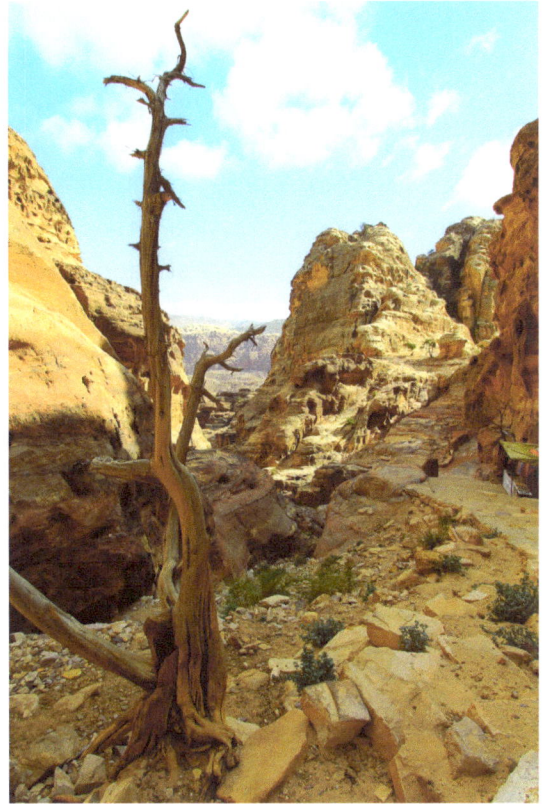

Remains of a tree in the hills of Petra

Persian pistachio (*Pistacia khinjuk*)

Closer to the ground, there are smaller shrubs and herbs scattered across the sandy soils of the ruins. An opportunistic shrub, mitnan (*Thymelaea hirsuta*), has evolved xerophytic characteristics that allow the plant to thrive in the harsh conditions. Above ground, *T. hirsuta* can be seen growing to two metres, but its extensive root system can reach depths of nearly four metres allowing the plant to capitalise on any moisture trapped deep within surrounding soils. In addition, *T. hirsuta* possesses leaves and flowers that are minuscule and succulent with a waxy coating, ensuring what little water the plant does secure is retained particularly effectively.

T. hirsuta is part of the often-toxic Thymelaeaceae family, but its inedibility does not detract from its value. The plant has long been used by the local Bedouins medicinally, and its fibrous bark has made it a desirable material in the production of ropes, twines, and paper. A poultice of ground *T. hirsuta* and salt is even used in traditional Bedouin veterinary practices to reduce miscarriage in camels.

In recent times, the plant has become the focus of research for its use in sustainable biodiesel production, so the species' inedibility looks inconsequential to its value. Also known as mitnan by the Bedouins and part of the same Thymelaceae family as *T. hirsuta* is *Daphne linearifolia*. A pretty shrub with ornamental potential, it is just as common around Petra and often used similarly.

It seems an unlikely destination to want to migrate to, but not all the plants vying for survival in Petra are native. Designated a UNESCO World Heritage site of paramount importance, the ancient city draws in hundreds of thousands of visitors from around the world each year, and foreign seeds have at times accompanied this traffic. Alien species often possess characteristics that allow them to survive and compete with local species. At Petra, the golden crown beard (*Verbesina encelioides*) is a vigorous example. This American intruder is allelopathic and secretes toxic phenolic compounds from its roots that displace native vegetation and eliminate competition.

There are also foreign plants in Petra and its surroundings that have been brought in intentionally. Tucked into pockets of soil in walls and around Bedouin dwellings, the brightly coloured flowers of bulbs brought back from travels can be seen by visitors journeying at the right time of the year. These gardens and the tendency of the local people to create them provide an insight into a Petra long forgotten.

Seeing green in a land of sand

Petra was not always crumbling, nor was the city dry and desolate. In fact, in its prime, the thriving Nabataean metropolis was home to up to thirty-thousand people. The Nabataeans were an ancient Arabian society credited with the creation of Petra, who amassed great wealth from the manipulation and control of ancient trade routes.

Thymelaea hirsuta flowers

Mitnan (*Daphne linearifolia*)

Sternbergia clusiana and leaves of *Drimia aphylla*

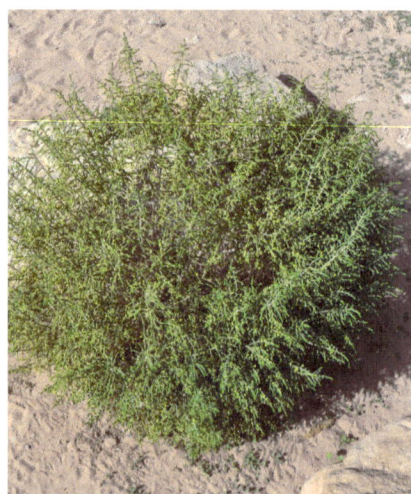

Thymelaea hirsuta a desert plant

Their knowledge of the region and its climate was unmatched during the time of the civilisation's dominance.

In addition to an understanding of the landscape and proficiency in trade, the Nabataeans' success was supported by a remarkable understanding of hydraulics. The members of the early society produced sophisticated water management systems which ensured a continuous, year-round water supply for the inhabitants of Petra and beyond. Through a hidden system of channels and dams carved into the sides of mountains, water could be routed several kilometres to below ground reservoirs and cisterns. When rain fell in the desert, the Nabataeans saved every drop. Additionally, the catchments ensured the city was kept safe from any flash floods.

Petra was a thriving city supporting crops and livestock at its peak, but beyond these essentials, ornamental horticulture was also embraced. Petra's gardens would likely have been designed to highlight the ancient Nabataean's triumph over the surrounding desert. They may have included elaborate water features unfathomable to those outside of the stone city's borders.

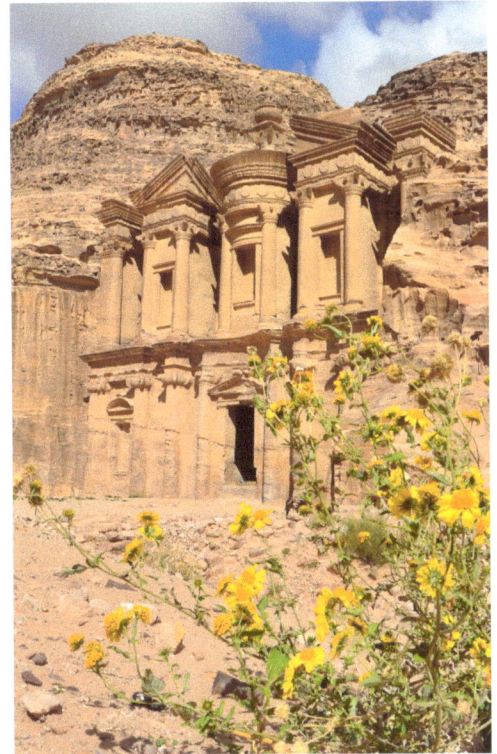

Invasive *Verbesina encelioides*

Engaged in a deep and historical relationship with water, it is not surprising that utilisation of the precious resource is still innovative in modern-day Jordan. In the south of the country lies the 'Valley of the Moon,' also known as Wadi Rum. It is an otherworldly landscape as harsh as any could be, where plants are few and far between. However, all is not as it seems in the deserts of Wadi Rum. Astonishingly, it is in this barren and repellent expanse of earth, that much of the country's fresh produce is farmed.

Nabataean ruins

Spanning hectare after hectare, perfect circles of green contrast against the desert sands. The geometrically perfect gardens are formed by vegetable crops grown under centre pivot irrigation; an irrigation system where a line of water emitters revolves around a central point. The result is a circular plot of compass-like precision. This form of production is also used in other areas of the Middle East and the farms, which can be seen from space, present horticultural landscapes that seem to blur the lines between science fiction and reality. Farming in the desert would seem implausible, if not impossible, but a key geographical feature under Wadi Rum has made the practice a reality.

A vast network of groundwater deposits known as the Saq-Ram aquifer system extends underneath the deserts of south-eastern Jordan into Saudi Arabia. The deposits provide much of Jordan's drinking water, and it has been the utilisation of this subterranean hydrologic resource that has made farming in Wadi Rum possible.

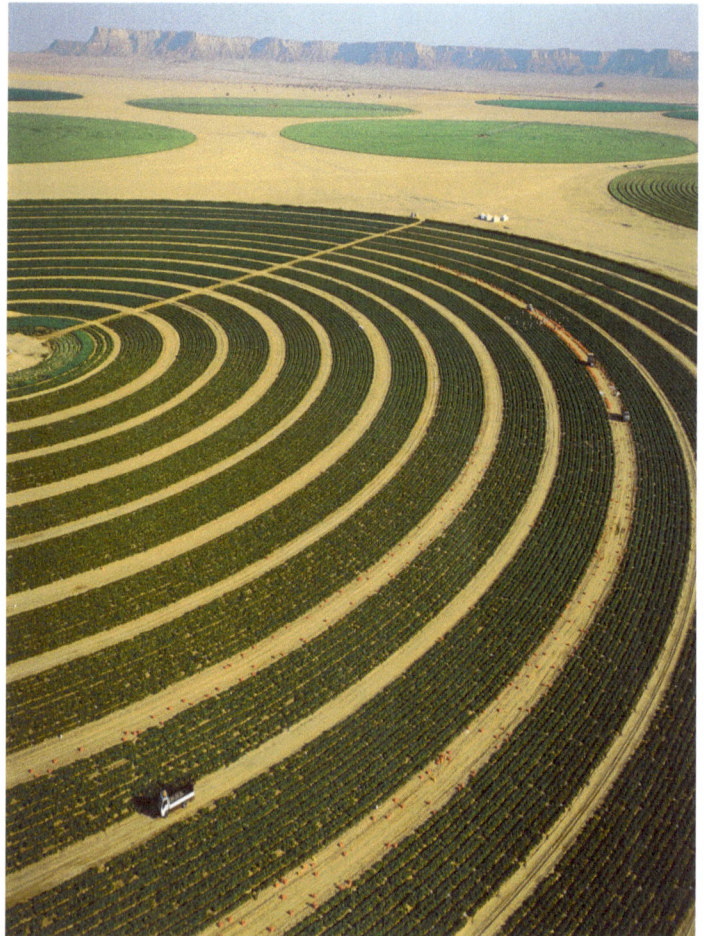

Desert farming utilising finite fossil water

Centre pivot farms can be seen from space in the Middle East

OFF THE GARDEN PATH

At its peak, Petra would have been an opulent oasis in the desert and a sight to behold. The hydraulic manipulation of the region's moisture allowed for the greening of a landscape where otherwise baked soil crumbles underfoot. Centuries later, the centre pivot farms of Wadi Rum are again only possible through hydraulic manipulation of the area's natural water sources. However, there is a fundamental difference between the farmers of today and the Nabataean masters of the Old World. A flaw, which, unfortunately, guarantees that these desert farms have a finite lifespan that is rapidly drawing to an end.

The Nabataeans developed a deep understanding of the desert climate and were able to capture, store and maximise any rainfall they received. Excess water was diverted from where it might otherwise have caused flood damage, and through extensive hydraulic infrastructure, the society thrived on the area's natural rainfall. The centre pivot farms of Wadi Rum instead utilise water from deep below the Earth's surface, and therein lies a problem. Some aquafers are naturally recharged after rain events, while others are not. Much of this farming relies on tapping into fossil deposits formed tens of thousands of years ago, which do not recharge and are quickly disappearing. In the face of a growing population and climate uncertainty, even the aquafers that do recharge are exploited too vigorously to have time to refill. It all points to a rather dire future for the desert nation, but other farms are appearing in the desert, farms that have managed to avoid a reliance on groundwater and just might hold the key to a sustainable future.

Wild fig *(Ficus palmata)* at Khazali Canyon in Wadi Rum

Date palm (*Phoenix dactylifera*) suited to desert farming

Leucaena flower (*Leucaena leucocephala*)

Swales dry out quickly without shade from larger plants

Greening the desert

Permaculture has found its way to Jordan. A concept that was initially developed in Australia in the nineteen-seventies, the merit of permaculture and its principles for production have seen the practice embraced worldwide. The idea integrates many elements and has been described in many ways. At its core, permaculture promotes the synthesis of ecology, geography, observation, and design, resulting in sustainable production and livelihoods.

While the concept of permaculture is recent by Jordanian standards, many of the horticultural techniques involved draw on the practices of traditional cultures, and some permaculture gardens probably display similarities to those grown by the Nabataeans of old. Ancient tried and tested agricultural techniques may need little improvement. Still, they can be enriched through a modern understanding of science, and it is a combination of these aspects that drives success in permaculture.

In Jordan, water is scarce, and the sun is relentless, so farmers need to prioritise these challenges. Swales assist in water capture to maximise the valuable resource for production, but without shade, much of this water would be lost to evaporation. Many of the swales at permaculture sites in Jordan are planted up with a mixture of valuable fruit trees, date palms (*Phoenix dactylifera*), and fast-growing plants in the legume family, including lebbeck trees (*Albizia lebbeck*), leucaenas (*Leucaena leucocephala*), and sesbans (*Sesbania sesban*). While the benefits of fruit trees are clear, the reason for planting legumes is a little less apparent.

The inclusion of diverse tree species lessens wind, stabilises soils, and provides shade but the planting of leguminous trees offers an additional benefit. Through a unique relationship with specialised bacteria that colonise their roots, many legumes can extract atmospheric nitrogen from the

OFF THE GARDEN PATH

air in soils and convert it into usable fertiliser. With their tendency for rapid growth, they can also be pruned hard several times a year to provide an organic mulch layer to cover bare soils.

Ordinarily, soil microbes deplete soils of nitrogen when breaking down woody mulch, which can cause deficiencies in crops. Leguminous species access and store nitrogen, which aids in composting organic matter. They are one of the most efficient assets for farmers wanting to rebuild soil health in the desert. Given time, swales become protected, soils improve, excellent crops are produced, and desertification can be stopped.

There are many tricks of the desert permaculture trade. Succulent groundcovers, including sun rose (*Aptenia cordifolia*) and pigface (*Carpobrotus edulis*), regulate soil temperatures, suppress weeds, and retain soil moisture. Monocultures are avoided to lessen the likelihood of pest outbreaks and minimise the risk of soils becoming depleted of any single nutrient. Polycultures are embraced, which include chickens and other animals to provide a source of plant nutrients. Soil health is paramount, with composting systems and worm farms regarded as particularly important, and other innovative closed-loop lifestyle practices are commonplace.

The permaculture sites of Jordan are making a shift from degenerative agriculture, where resources are consumed without long-term foresight, to regenerative agriculture. Across the world, desertification is increasing, so it is encouraging to know this phenomenon can not only be reduced but can be reversed with a little human intervention and perseverance.

Horticultural operations around the globe can inspire wonder, sometimes at the expense of the planet. However, displaying successful regenerative horticulture in one of the driest places on Earth, Jordan's desert permaculture gardens offer a green wonder producing a rare environmental surplus.

Woman holding a harvest of chillies (*Capsicum frutescens*)

Gardens of Ethics and Ecology
The Relais and Chateaux Museum Hotel
Cappadocia, Turkey

Culture with cuisine to match

As the geographical crossroads between Europe and Asia, Turkey has long been a centre for global commerce. From its time as an integral part of the 'Silk Road' trade route to the present day, there is very little that hasn't been bought or sold through Turkish trade, and a great deal of what has changed hands has come as a result of horticultural enterprises throughout the ages.

Actually, an ancient network of passages, the Silk Road trade routes that linked the Old World regions, were of unparalleled importance for centuries, playing a significant role in forming the world in which we live today. From exotic animals, plants,

Baklava stall in Istanbul

textiles, and spices, to porcelain, dyes, medicines, and jewels, there wasn't much of value that didn't travel the Silk Road, and the one thing almost all traders had in common was a thoroughfare through Turkey.

In recent times the country has become a modern and vibrant melting pot of activity, thriving on tourism and difficult to visit without getting caught up in the history, culture, and cuisine on display. Whether it is the iconic architecture, bartering at a bazaar, or sampling delicious desserts along the famous

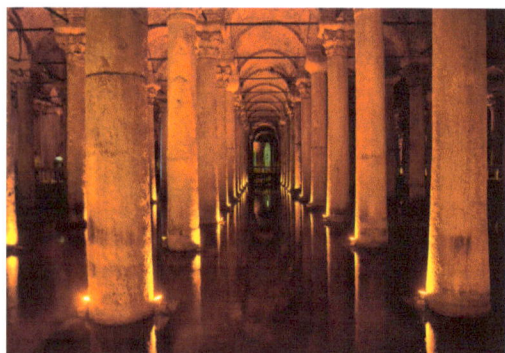
Ancient Basilica Cistern built in the sixth century

Istiklal Street in Istanbul, a visit to Turkey simultaneously induces appreciation of the past, enthusiasm for the present, and anticipation for the future.

From baklava to şiş kebap, food plays a crucial role in Turkish culture. Influenced by the historical-cultural interactions of the Silk Road and its time within the once expansive Ottoman Empire, the country's cuisine is a fusion of Central Asian, Middle Eastern, Eastern European, Armenian, and Balkan flavours that are somehow distinctly Turkish.

In addition to treats like almond halva and Turkish delight, some culinary offerings found in the region are unlike anything offered anywhere else in the world, except perhaps in a few of the neighbouring countries that were also once part of the Ottoman Empire. One such offering is Turkish ice cream or 'salepli dondurma,' characterised by its resistance to melting, firm texture, and chewiness compared to the ice cream traditionally consumed in the West.

These qualities are achieved by using a unique blend of ingredients, including mastic – a plant resin derived from the

Istanbul by night

Orchis mascula **one of the orchids used in salep**

mastic tree (*Pistacia lentiscus*) and salep powder – a starchy flour made from the tubers (underground storage organs) of several types of orchid, including *Orchis, Ophrys,* and *Dactylorhiza* species. Salep is also the name given to the traditional Turkish milk drink consisting of salep powder as its key ingredient. Unfortunately, the popularity of salep has led to a severe decline in orchid populations, with some facing extinction. As a result, several species are now totally protected, and salep itself is banned from export beyond Turkish borders to curb demand.

It is not hard to understand how orchid populations would be impacted, considering that producing just one kilogram of salep flour requires around four thousand orchid tubers, which take up to eight years to grow to a sufficient size to harvest. Salep is indeed a Turkish rarity.

Cup of Turkish salep

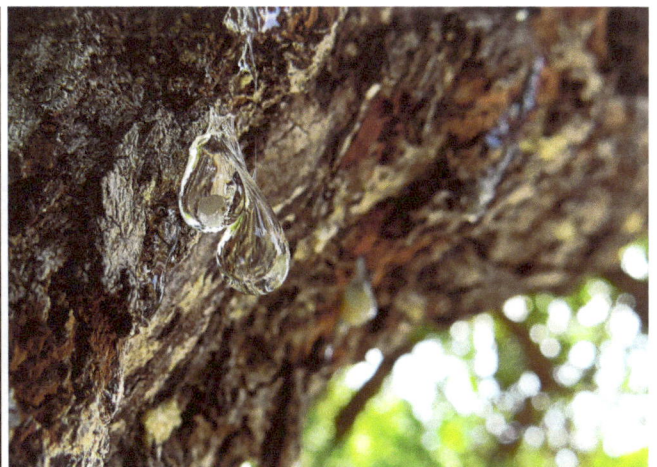

Mastic tree *(Pistacia lentiscus)*

Productive lands open to change

Another contributing factor in the diversity of Turkish cuisine is the extensive range of produce farmed across the country, particularly in the region of Anatolia. Turkey has a total land area of nearly eighty million hectares, encompassing meadows, forests, lakes, and settled areas. It also has more than eight million hectares of arable land. The quality and quantity of the produce the land allows for contributes to the sense of decadence imparted by Turkish dining. This arable land is also a significant reason the country is a world leader in the production of many fruit crops, including apricots, cherries, figs, and grapes. In fact, Turkey's horticultural production, in general, is quite astounding, with farmers harvesting close to fifteen million tons of fruit and thirty million tons of vegetables annually.

Dried orchid tubers used in salep

However, rather than production on a mass scale, most farms in Turkey are quite small, at around five hectares on average. Unfortunately, although the farms are small, past farming practices adopted from the dawn of the twentieth century have impacted the environment. In Turkey, as echoed around the developed world, intensifying production using chemical fertilisers, pesticides, and inept irrigation methods is now accepted as ecologically and economically unsustainable.

Fairy chimneys and farming in Cappadocia

As a result, many Turkish farmers are striving to create and foster healthy agro-ecosystems that incorporate sustainable practices at all stages of the supply chain, from production to plate. Perfectly suited to the smaller-sized farms, the move away from chemical reliance is now improving employment opportunities and securing incomes in the country.

Many of the projects have become completely organic, presenting enviable quality and characteristics that are highly sought after abroad. As a result, Turkey boasts a healthy export industry, but much of the produce stays within the country, ensuring Turkish ingredients are the freshest possible. By prioritising locavore market chains, farmers attract visitors from across the country and overseas, pursuing the exceptional produce offered throughout this unique part of the world.

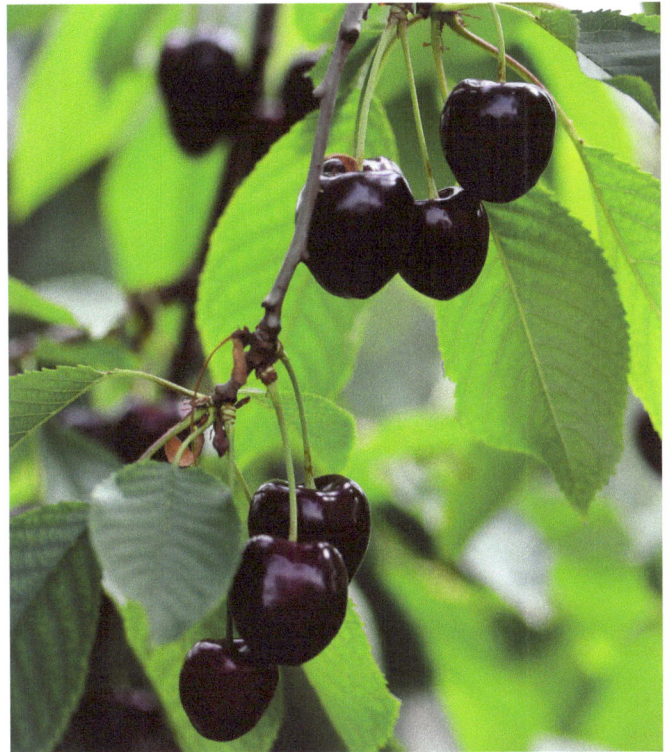

Turkey's biggest exports include cherries *(Prunus avium)*

In a lavish twist of fortune, some of Turkey's finest examples of paddock to plate farming and premium produce just happen to be accompanied by one of the most picturesque landscapes on Earth – Cappadocia.

Imbrignite rock formations

When conditions are right the surreal landscape of Cappadocia is accompanied by hundreds of hot air balloons

Aerial view of Cappadocia region

A geological fantasy realm

Deep in the heart of Anatolia lies a region possessing a landscape so surreal, it appears as if it has been handcrafted to act as the backdrop for a sylphid's fairy tale. Ancient Cappadocia is as historically significant as it is beautiful, and crowds flock from across the planet to experience its spellbinding hills, valleys, caves, and rock formations. The sheer scale of visitors to the area is illustrated daily at the break of dawn when masses of hot air balloons take to the skies, crowding the horizon and treating lucky passengers to a bird's eye view of the dreamlike expanse below.

The charm of Cappadocia comes from a unique blend of geological activity and weathering combined with eons of human intervention. It is thought around sixty million years ago, ancient volcanic eruptions covered the area in blankets of ash and lava, which in turn formed a layer of rock known as ignimbrite, tens of metres thick. Over the years since wind and water have eroded softer materials leaving the harder elements behind to form the otherworldly landscapes of today.

As far back as the Palaeolithic era, early humans had discovered the soft and easily worked formations and following nature's lead, proceeded to tunnel entire cities into the rocks, complete with living quarters, places of worship, stables, and storehouses. Some city complexes even incorporated hidden underground networks thought to house tens of thousands of people. Far from being abandoned, many of the structures are still used as dwellings today.

The landscape of Cappadocia commands attention but the natural flora of the region is quite unassuming. The semi-arid Mediterranean climate fosters mostly herbaceous steppe vegetation, though moisture retained in deeper valleys also allows some larger species to thrive.

While the surrounding geology may distract from the subtle and easily missed vegetation, many of the plants of Cappadocia display adaptations for survival as impressive as those of the civilisations that crafted the landscape. Among such plants are several milk vetch species (*Astragalus* spp.), some of which are glacial steppe relics left behind as species diversified after the last ice age. It is no wonder, considering the seed can remain viable for over one hundred and thirty years.

Many have been used in traditional medicine for centuries, but species of milk vetch are not alone in their medicinal value. When investigating the landscape further, it quickly becomes apparent that Cappadocia is home to many useful plant species. The scrappy form and delicate flowers of leadwort (*Plumbago europaea*) are not nearly as showy as its domesticated cousins, but *P. europaea* is not utilised for its ornamental value in Cappadocia. Across the Mediterranean, this plant has long been used medicinally, for everything from treating inflammation and

Common immortelle (*Xeranthemum annuum*)

Leadwort (*Plumbago europaea*)

Alkanet (*Anchusa undulata*)

A milk vetch species (*Astragalus sp.*)

sciatica, to aiding with respiratory disorders. Possessing proven anti-bacterial properties, it has even been investigated for use as a self-deodorising dye in the textile industry.

Almost as inconspicuous, shrubby members of the genus *Anchusa* also frequent the landscape. Several species have been used traditionally to assist the healing of wounds, as diuretics, analgesics, and even as sedatives. Closer to the ground, the common immortelle (*Xeranthemum annuum*), a type of everlasting daisy, is also widespread and reported to have been used to soothe burns and relieve toothaches when mixed with tobacco in traditional Turkish folk medicine.

First appearing somewhat desolate and not somewhere you would want to fall ill, Cappadocia is actually a veritable pharmacy!

Dwellings carved into the soft and easily worked rock formations

A garden experience that delivers thrice

Although its appearance is dominated by expansive pink and pastel ignimbrite rock, punctuated with thousands of the signature formations known as fairy chimneys, the landscape of Cappadocia is far from barren. On the contrary, it exhibits a beautiful collection of green spaces, from orchards to formal gardens. However, the water here is precious. With an annual rainfall of around only four hundred millimetres, plants would be largely confined to valleys and the banks of seasonal streams without human influence. To remedy this dilemma, Cappadocians throughout the ages have altered the area's natural hydrology. Water has been cleverly diverted from areas of surplus to where it has been lacking. This has increased productive land and reduced the risk of excess water, which could wash away fertile and productive valley soils during times of flooding.

Tunnelling subterranean aqueducts throughout the area's stone cities achieved this feat in hydraulic engineering of the Middle Ages. The size and scale of the tunnels are extraordinary, and the remains of many are still intact today. The most significant known extends to a total length of nearly four kilometres and incorporates over fifty separate surface connections to cisterns, fountains, and wells.

In present-day Cappadocia, water is still piped long distances. However, it is now sourced through bores in addition to rainwater capture and with the adoption of modern drip irrigation systems in the area, is dispersed far more efficiently. So efficiently, that with its already fertile volcanic soils just waiting on moisture, Cappadocia is set to considerably increase its production capacity over the coming years.

With a supply of water secured, amenity and kitchen gardens have followed, and some of the best examples are displayed by the region's numerous hotels. Many draw in visitors with their views, others with

View from the Relais and Chateaux Museum Hotel garden

Purposely placed historical garden ornaments

their rare and exotic fruit varieties, but few compare with what can be found at the Relais and Chateaux Museum Hotel in the popular town of Göreme.

As akin to a museum as it is to a hotel, everything about this site has been designed to enhance the charm of Cappadocia, and the facility's ornamental gardens are no exception. An impressive collection of Persian, Ottoman, and Roman artefacts have been purposefully placed throughout the hotel's interior and spill out into the gardens among lush roses, providing an instant air of historical romance. In addition, the hilltop location allows for both sunrise and sunset views over the surrounding landscape, and as an amenity garden experience, this one is hard to beat.

Live peacocks add to the garden's charm

While the ornamental aspects of the gardens are unique, they are just one element of the appeal in this botanical encounter. The site also features a kitchen garden situated in the shadows of the fairy chimneys, which has been designed to foster and showcase ecologically sound production practices. This venture takes the locavore principles embraced across much of Turkey and condenses them into an easily accessed, informative, and well-rounded experience for its visitors. Guests can wander the garden to pick and sample whatever organic produce is in season.

One of the most popular activities on offer for visitors is learning how to cook Turkish cuisine firsthand and a trip to the gardens to gather ingredients is a must before starting in the kitchen. The gardens produce fresh fruit, vegetables and flowers that also supply a bounty of pollen for the bees that contribute to the site's organic honey production. Cooking Turkish cuisine often requires eggs, and coming straight from the garden's free-range chickens, eggs don't get fresher. The

Cappadocian market

benefits of the chickens are threefold. They produce eggs, fertiliser and contribute to chemical-free pest control, which assist in the closed-loop organic productivity of the project.

If a visit to the ecological gardens doesn't yield the ingredients a recipe calls for, then a trip to a traditional Cappadocian market will. Here farmers and market gardeners from across the region regularly gather to offer their products for sale. It is this regularity that ensures the produce is the freshest possible. Through this support of local employment, markets, and farmers, the Relais and Chateaux Museum Hotel highlights the third and final drawcard in its horticultural endeavours - an ethos of ethical production.

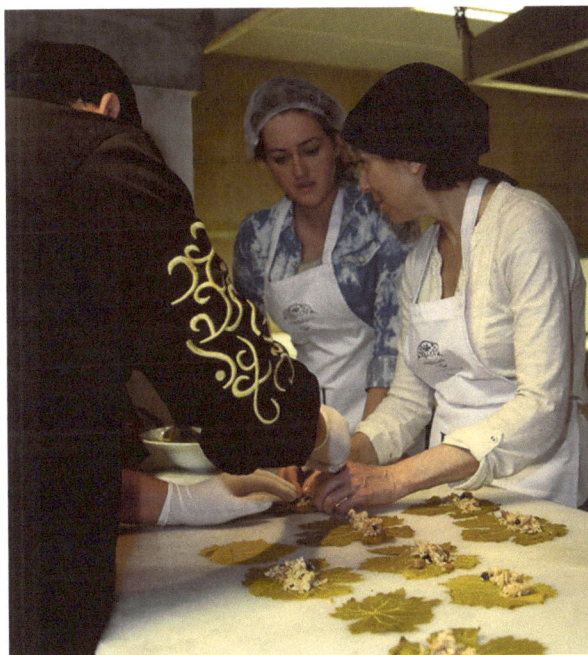

Guests learning how to cook Turkish cuisine

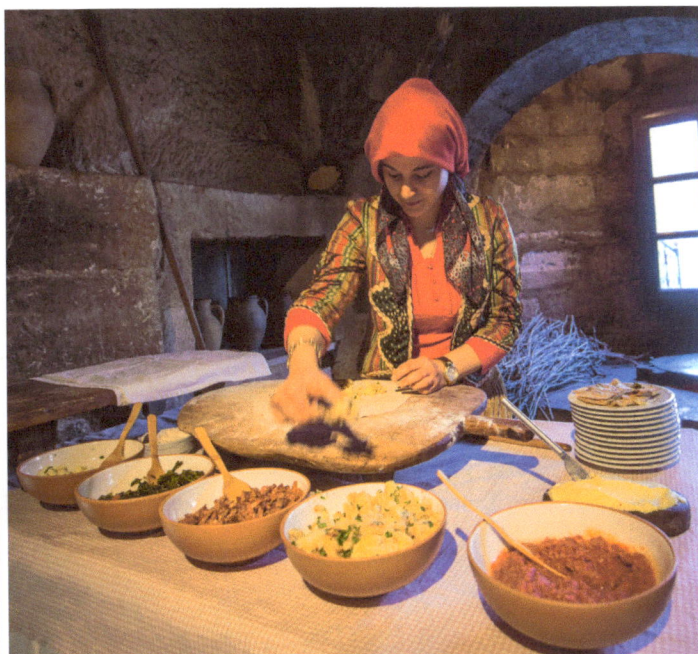

Fresh produce transformed into traditional dishes

Staff inspecting ripening fruit

Historically Cappadocia has been important in areas from commerce to religion, but the region is now primarily driven by tourism, and in addition to sightseeing, two horticultural niches appeal to visitors - ecotourism and agrotourism. With its kitchen garden focussed on ecological balance, the hotel encompasses agro and ecotourism aspects, but at two hundred acres, it is the hotel's nearby farming project that showcases ethical production. At the farm, everything is geared toward benefitting the community and keeping things local. Accessible with the aid of a quick four-wheel-drive trip, the site nurtures some of the region's best examples of ecologically and ethically grown crops. From apples and almonds to strawberries and walnuts, the orchards foster an extensive variety of produce tended by local workers.

Cappadocia is also renowned for its wine, and a considerable portion of the farm's land is dedicated to viticulture. The grapes that are grown don't travel far and are instead used to produce the region's very own, exclusive range of wines and a Turkish delicacy, 'pekmez'.

Grapes being picked to produce the hotel's wine

Pekmez is a molasses-like syrup made through the reduction of grape juice, and while a delicacy for the rest of the world, it is a standard ingredient in Turkish cuisine. In Cappadocia, the process of making the syrup remains traditional and is a social affair for local women who happily gather to spend a day conversing while boiling down the fruit. The social aspect of production can also be witnessed during the creation of another of Cappadocia's famous delicacies, sun-dried apricots.

Fresh apricots (*Prunus armeniaca*)

Cappadocians take the process of drying apricots very seriously, and during this season, things are not done by halves but rather in tonnes, with drying grounds spanning hundreds of metres. Intense flavours are achieved within the fruit when left to dry in the plentiful sun of the Cappadocian summer. Famous worldwide, the sun-dried apricots are then stored and used out of season or exported to fortunate markets across the globe.

Dried apricots are also the core ingredient in kaymakli kayisi tatlisi (Turkish stuffed apricots). For this culinary treat,

Kayisi tatlisi (Turkish stuffed apricots)

they are reconstituted before being filled with kaymak (a soft cheese produced using buffalo milk), drissled in syrup, and garnished with pistachios. The resulting snack is slightly sweet, salty, creamy, and sour all at once.

Apricots drying in the Cappadocian sun

Whether grown in its gardens and farm or sourced through local markets, much of the produce to be experienced at the Relais and Chateaux Museum Hotel is supplied by local producers. This in turn supports the region and its inhabitants economically and sustainably.

From a gardener's perspective, a great deal has been accomplished within this venture. The ornamental gardens illustrate that an amenity garden can extend well beyond displaying plants and can be used to impart cultural and historical meaning with spellbinding results. By embracing ecologically sound principles and highlighting sustainable practices, an everyday kitchen garden has been transformed into a highly sought-after locavore dining experience, and a productive orchard driven by ethics has proven no less successful after putting people first.

It is for these reasons and more that these gardens in magical Cappadocia certainly warrant a place among the world's most wondrous.

Apple tree framing Goreme Valley

Gardening for Production
The Floating Gardens of Inle Lake
Nyaungshwe Valley, Myanmar

A mysterious land steeped in history

Earth is a planet where natural wonders are offered in abundance, from plants and animals to geology and landscapes. Countries the world over possess jewels of nature and encompass rich histories of how these wonders have been influenced, for better or worse, through the arrival of human beings. There are ancient stories handed down in every culture, but among the most mysterious is the history of the Southeast Asian country of Myanmar.

Myanmar is a sovereign state bordered by Bangladesh, India, China, Laos, and Thailand. Many aspects of the country's past are complex, tragic, and even heartbreaking, but despite this, its people are warm, welcoming, and its scenery breathtaking. Known as the golden country, the landscapes of Myanmar are peppered with ornate pagodas proudly swathed in gold, so numerous it is impossible to enter the country without catching a glimpse of them, towering above the tropical greenery. Taking in these pagodas, one quickly gains an insight into the significance of religion and particularly Buddhism, in the region. However, when discovering the less conspicuous and crumbling ruins of ancient temples in areas like the Bagan Plateau in the nation's Mandalay region and the Nyaung Ohak complex in the Shan State to the east, the true historic scale of Myanmar's Buddhist roots becomes apparent.

Visitors to these ruins are transported back in time to a kingdom long abandoned. It is thought that Bagan originated as a small settlement in the late ninth century and, over several hundred years, grew to become the capital of the ancient Kingdom of Pagan - a major centre for religion that attracted

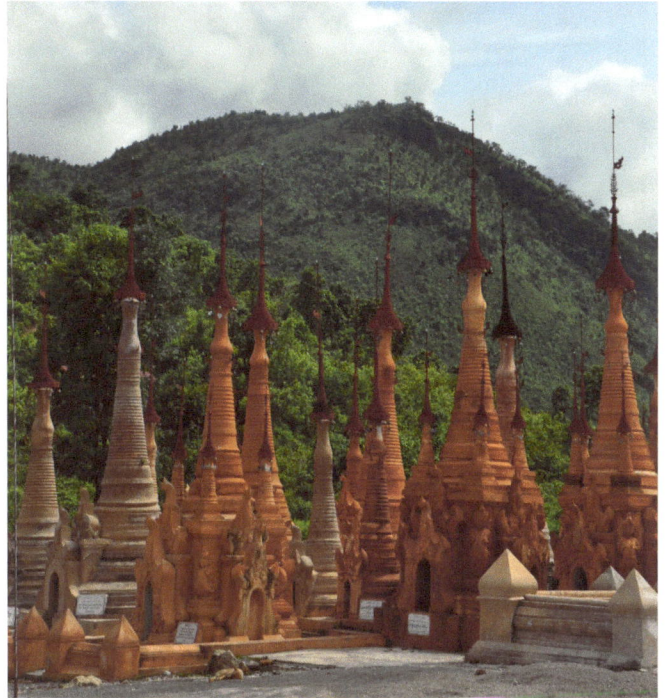

Recently built pagodas at the Nyaung Ohak complex

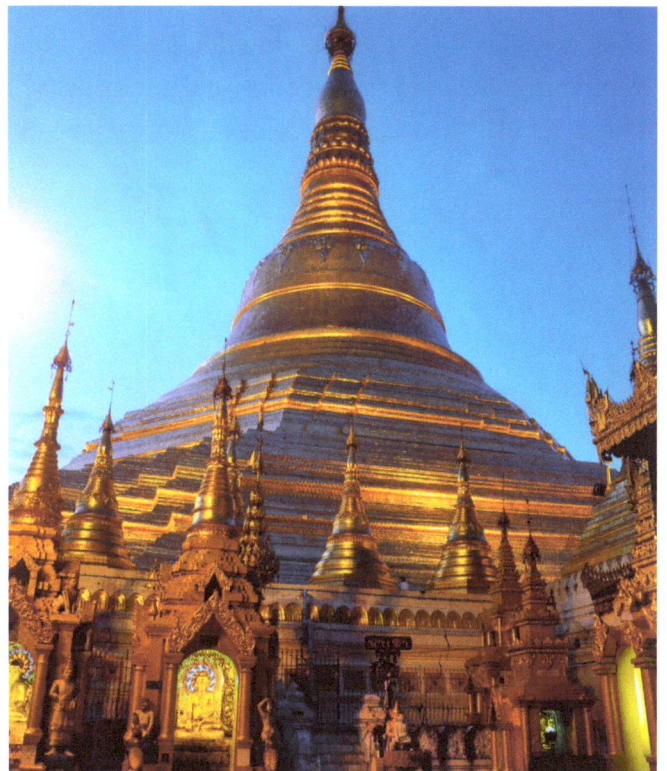

The Golden Dagon Pagoda, Yangon

Nyaung Ohak, the surreal jungle-village of crumbling temples

monks and scholars from across Southeast Asia. At its peak, between the eleventh and twelfth centuries CE, the area presented over ten thousand Buddhist stupas, temples, and monasteries. Highlighting the region's influence, it was also Pagan royalty that commissioned the now crumbling pagodas at the Nyaung Ohak complex, over three hundred kilometres away. Both sites have since been subject to centuries of weathering, including earthquakes and floods. As a result, today many pagodas are all but reclaimed by the jungle. To visit these sites provides a surreal insight into Myanmar's prodigious past and an appreciation

Vegetation reclaiming stupa

Ancient figure of Buddha at Nyaung Ohak

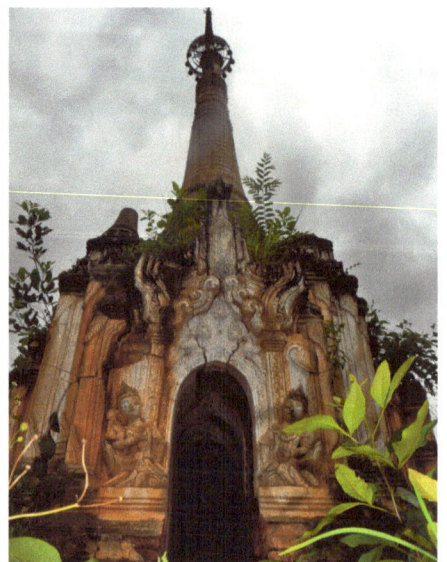

Weathered stupa at Nyaung Ohak

Bagan Plateau is home to over two thousand Buddhist temples and pagodas

of nature's ability to transform hundreds of years of human interference into obscurity.

Humans had been present in Myanmar long before the rise and fall of Bagan, and archaeological evidence suggests that *Homo sapiens* lived in the area as early as twenty-five thousand years ago. There is also strong evidence to suggest the domestication of plants and animals as far back as ten thousand years BCE. With this early domestication of plants, the region's first gardeners were born.

Horticultural diversity in the tropics

With a lineage of gardeners spanning millennia and the diversity of over one hundred recognised ethnic groups, it is no wonder production horticulture and agriculture drive the region's economy. The classic rice paddies seen across much of Southeast Asia are displayed throughout the country. They account for about half of all agricultural land, with the agricultural industry employing around a third of the country's

Traditional agriculture can be seen across Myanmar

Dragon fruit (*Selenicereus undatus*) and dried eel found at a local market

workforce. However, the scale of rice farming is by no means an indicator of the diversity of crops raised in the country, and a visit to any local market uncovers a myriad of culinary treasures.

Myanmar can be divided into three agricultural zones. The delta plays host to flooded rice paddies. The dry zone is primarily irrigated rice, sugarcane, legumes, corn, and other staples, while the hill and plateau regions are used for forestry and cultivation of various crops using shifting agriculture techniques. A variety of tropical fruit also spans these regions, from plantain (*Musa × paradisiaca*) and durian (*Durio zibethinusto*) to mangosteen (*Garcinia mangostana*) and dragon fruit (*Selenicereus undatus*).

The horticulture industry in Myanmar is not restricted to food crops, and as Buddhism is so deeply rooted in the culture, there is a huge market for cut flowers. The flowers are used as offerings when the country's inhabitants visit any of the religious sites by which Myanmar is so clearly defined. It is commonplace to grow and sell garden chrysanthemums (*Chrysanthemum × morifolium*) and zinnias

Cut flowers used on mass in Buddhist rituals

OFF THE GARDEN PATH

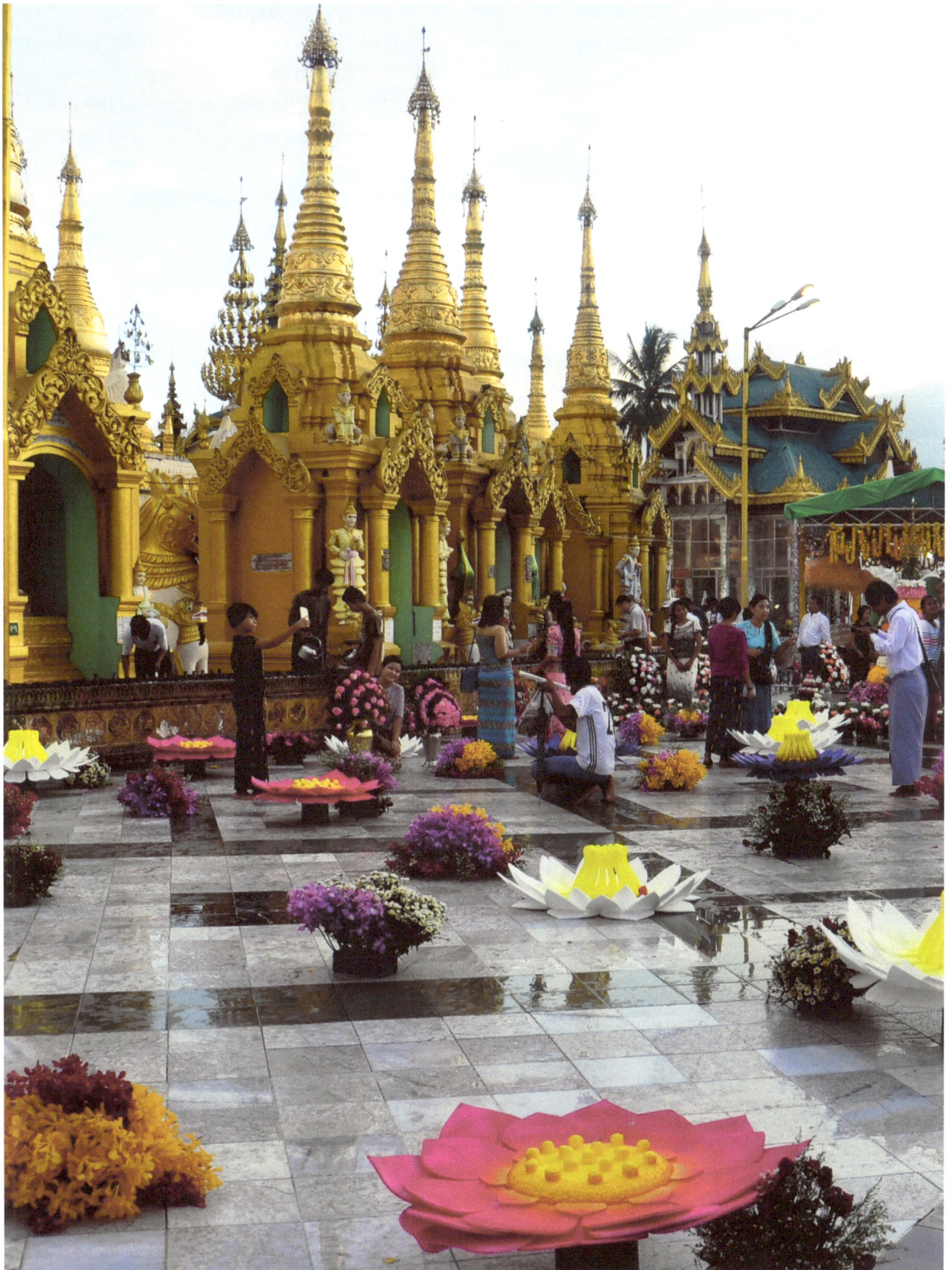

Flowers play a huge part in the rituals held at the Golden Dagon Pagoda

(*Zinnia elegans*), especially in rural areas, but a diversity of species can be found in the cities. Flower markets offer everything from roses (*Rosa* spp.), gladioli (*Gladiolus* spp.), and flamingo lilies (*Anthurium andraeanum*) to exotic specimens, including thazin orchids (*Bulbophyllum auricomum*) and padauk (*Pterocarpus macrocarpus*), Myanmar's floral emblem. The prevalence of flower markets and the diversity of species they offer demonstrate how important horticulture is in the country. Whether in temples or offices, the picturesque scenes in the golden country drip with botanical colour. Around ninety percent of the nation's floriculture production is used for religious purposes. With a population of over fifty million (the majority of whom make several offerings to Buddha each day), the production achieved by Burmese farmers has to be incredibly efficient to meet demand.

Also driven by the Burmese commitment to Buddhism are the numerous species of *Syzygium* grown in the region, regarded as having religious significance. This is probably due to their part in the story of Buddha's first spiritual experience, which occurred under a rose apple (*Syzygium jambos*). As the story goes, it was under the shade of the rose apple, watching his father work, that Buddha drifted into the happiness and pleasure of his first meditation. The Burmese know the story well, but for much of the world, Buddha is better known for an association with the bodhi tree (*Ficus religiosa*). As hinted to by its species name, the bodhi tree has long been of similar importance. In a more frequently told chapter of Buddhism, under this tree, Buddha is said to have surpassed meditation and gained true enlightenment.

Jambolan (*Syzygium cumini*) is among the other prized species in the *Syzygium* genus, and striking readily from root cuttings, is commonplace at local markets. Often these cuttings have a permanent presence

Jambolan (*Syzygium cumini*) are commonplace at local markets

in buildings and households, providing a long-lived cut foliage of sorts. Unfortunately, this longevity and ease in propagation make *S. cumini* a significant weed in many countries. Other tree species cultivated across Myanmar include Burmese teak (*Tectona grandis*) and rubber (*Hevea brasiliensis*), as well as several useful timber species, but perhaps the most interesting are the trees synonymous with the Burmese people themselves - thanaka.

Thanaka and traditional medicine

It has been said that though it is a country of immense beauty, the most charismatic feature of Myanmar does not appear in the landscape but on the faces of the people. Entering the region, it is not long before you are greeted with a smiling face adorned with a cream-coloured paste often ornately applied to the nose and cheeks. This is the quintessential Burmese cosmetic, thanaka. Thanaka comes from the bark and wood fibres of several trees indigenous to the Southeast

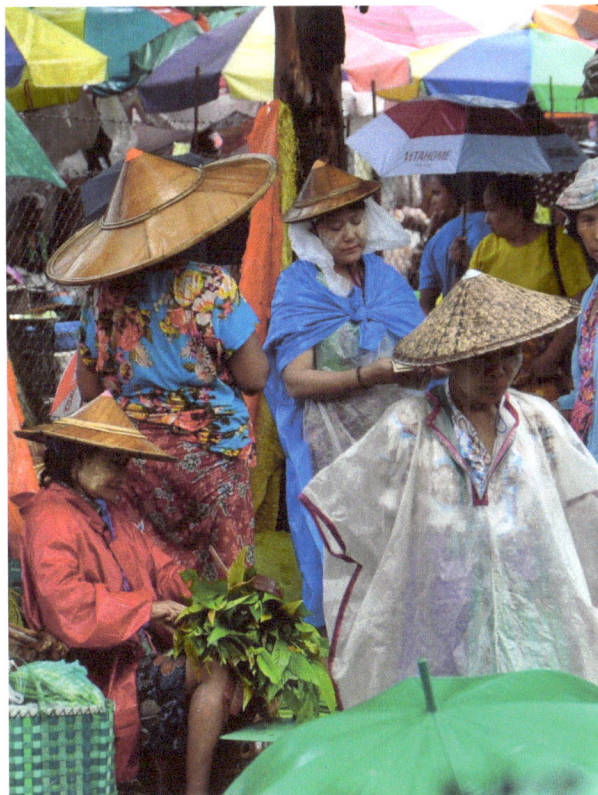

Burmese women at a local produce market

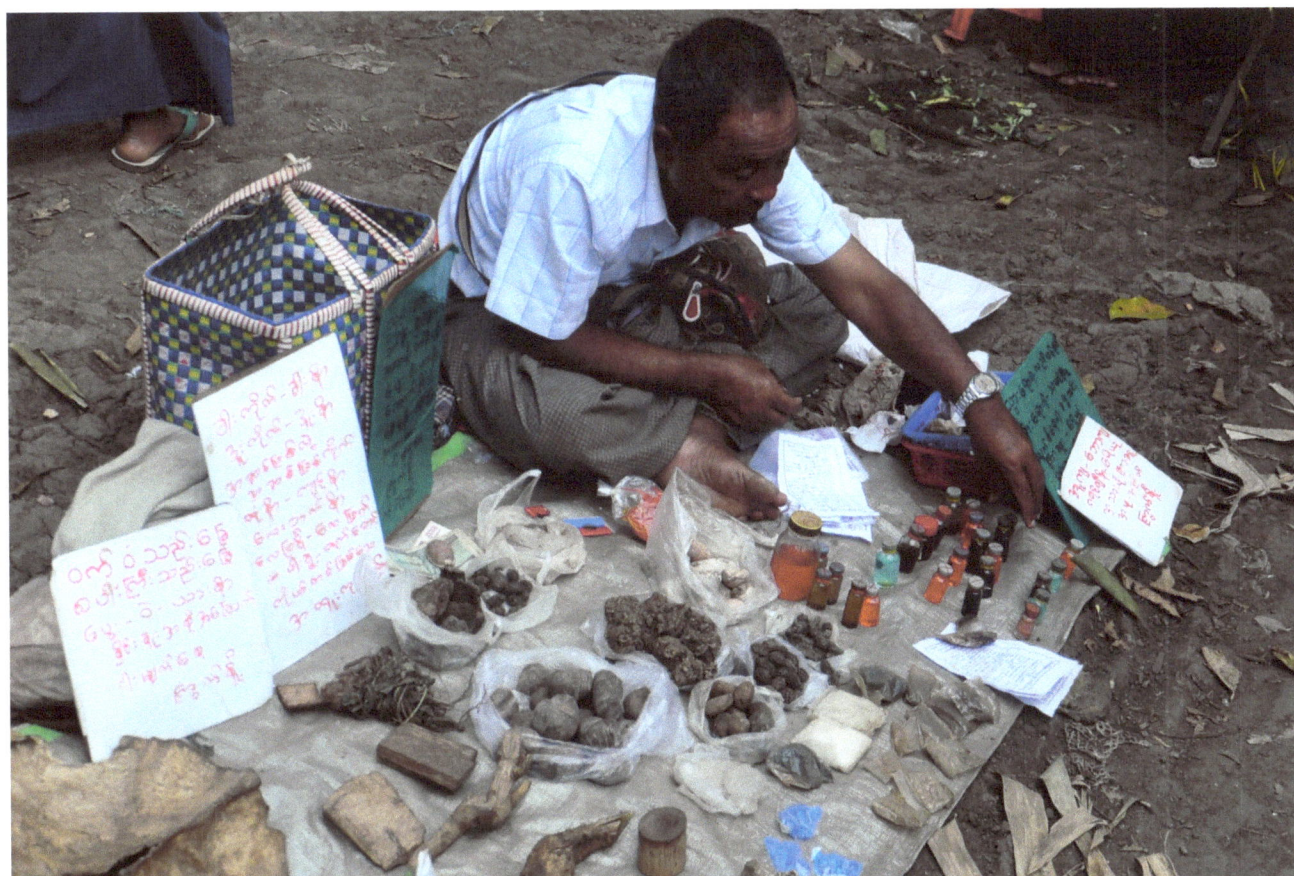

Maintaining tradition, medicines derived from plants and animals are sold at markets across Myanmar

Village buildings can be found both on and around Inle Lake

Asian regions. The most notable species are *Limonia acidissima* and *Hesperethusa crenulata*, which share the common name of thanaka.

In a relatively simple daily task, thanaka cream is produced by manually grinding branch sections of these species against a circular abrasive disk or 'kyauk pyin'. The apparatus catches the resulting slurry, which is then applied to the face as a multi-purpose cream. Possessing benefits said to include everything from sun protection and providing basic makeup to anti-aging and skin cleansing, thanaka is thought to have been used for over two thousand years.

In recent times the benefits of thanaka have been substantiated by several scientific studies. The product contains two active ingredients, coumarin, and marmesin. Coumarin has proven antibacterial,

Intha gardener collecting aquatic plants

Eichhornia crassipes is the basis of the floating gardens

Floating gardens constructed with decomposing weeds and water hyacinth

antifungal, and antioxidant properties, while marmesin serves as a form of natural UV-A protection. Due to these findings, the product has gained the attention of major cosmetic brands, seeking to commercialise pastes and powders to be processed for global distribution.

While there aren't many traditional remedies as popular in the country as thanaka, values, and beliefs in traditional medicine are still widely upheld. In markets across the country, vendors can be found displaying eclectic mixes of naturally derived concoctions and tinctures, still to be researched, so there are likely many more beneficial compounds in use yet to be commercialised from the region.

Innovative aquatic production

Looking at its past, it is undeniable that a history of gardening runs deep in Myanmar. However, one of the most remarkable of its horticultural enterprises is also one of the most recent. Not far from the pagoda ruins of Nyaung Ohak extends one of the country's largest lakes. The body of water spans well over one hundred square kilometres, and it is here in the Shan State that people come from all over the world to see the legendary floating gardens of Inle Lake.

A Pao woman selling tomatoes

Produce is transported across the Inle Lake daily by long boats

The exact size of the lake is hard to calculate as the lines between land and water are constantly changing. However, the sprawling networks of plants floating on aquatic garden beds are known to occupy over seven thousand acres of the lake's surface area. These beds are a feat in human innovation, made of decomposed plant material and the floating aquatic herb, water hyacinth (*Eichhornia crassipes*). The process of preparing each bed is time-consuming and laborious. The water hyacinth must first be trapped between floating bamboo frames and topped with various organic matter, including the lake's

Tomatoes growing on Inle Lake account for sixty percent of the country's production

Intha woman weaving lotus fibers into a fine thread

Sacred lotus (*Nelumbo nucifera*)

aquatic grasses, before being left to decompose to form an ideal growing substrate. Unfortunately, the water hyacinth is not indigenous to the lake. Since being introduced, it has offset its benefits with pernicious problems. It often clogs the lake's networks of canals and threatens the area's biodiversity. However, for creating a floating growing medium, its merit is unrivalled.

The Inthe ethnic group who inhabit the lake and its surroundings in stilt houses tend to the variety of vegetables grown on the buoyant beds. The crops are diverse, from cucurbits to sunflowers, but much of the lake is used to produce tomatoes. Over sixty thousand tonnes of the fruit are harvested annually, about sixty percent of the country's total tomato production.

Lake inhabitants processing tobacco and spices into cigars

While the floating gardens are as unique as Myanmar itself, the concept of floating farms has been around for centuries. It is thought that the Aztecs developed a system of floating gardens around the tenth century CE, and similar gardens have been documented in China from at least the thirteenth century. In comparison, the gardens on Inle Lake are far more recent and were only introduced in the nineteen sixties, though the principles remain the same as those used in the ancient gardens.

The frequent traffic of long-tail boats heavily laden with tomatoes on Inle Lake alludes to the fact that tomato farming is the principal venture in the area. Still, it is far from the only horticultural industry in operation. Store owners catering to tourist traffic produce an assortment of unique products. Some offer textiles made from water lotus (*Nelumbo nucifera*) fibres, carefully spun into silken threads before undergoing a complex weaving process. Others use tobacco and local ingredients to create distinctive Shan State cigars. Produced in the absence of soil, the abundant offerings found throughout the lake's gardens are nothing short of amazing.

Whether it is the tapestries of vivid greens that adorn the rolling hills, a sunset over the shimmering aquatic villages, or the smiles and hospitality of the people, this is a place that stays in the hearts of travellers – the scenery sublime and the people inspiring. Rich in cultural and botanical history, Myanmar and the productive floating gardens of Inle Lake certainly deserve their place as a green wonder of the world.

Sunset over the floating gardens of Inle Lake

Horticulture for Preservation
Raising the Giants of the Tropics
Malay Archipelago, South Pacific Ocean

Islands that breed biodiversity

Islands, and the extent to which they are isolated, have had a remarkable effect on evolution and species diversification over the millennia. From the lemurs of Madagascar to the finches of the Galapagos Islands documented by Charles Darwin, islands foster cradles of biodiversity. However, there is one island that has produced more species than any other. An island that is home to an estimated fifteen thousand species of plants and many of the world's most unusual animals.

Wagler's pit viper (*Tropidolaemus wagleri*)

Borneo is Asia's largest island and forms part of the Malay Archipelago in the far southwestern Pacific Ocean. At an estimated one hundred and fifty million years of age, the rugged landmass also encompasses the world's oldest rainforest, which at one point covered around seventy-five percent of the island's surface. This combination of maturity and size has allowed the development of an unmatched richness of species that has cemented Borneo as a must-visit destination for every naturalist's bucket list. Throughout its lifetime, the rainforest has experienced floods, glaciation, and droughts, all driving evolution, and speciation. So, it is no wonder several portions of the island have been deemed UNESCO World Heritage sites due to their biological importance.

Borneo's moist tropical climate fuels species diversification

Curious orangutan in Bornean jungle

The complex environmental niches created in this biologically diverse setting and the plants and animals that have evolved to fill them have ensured that Borneo sports some of Earth's most unusual life forms. The species found in this untamed pocket of the planet are like nothing else, from the well-known Bornean orangutans (*Pongo pygmaeus*), distinct proboscis monkeys (*Nasalis larvatus*), and rainforest pygmy elephants (*Elephas maximus borneensis*) to deadly arboreal snakes, endemic cats, and the world's longest stick insect (*Phobaeticus chani*).

Plants, too, have developed into a myriad of forms to succeed in every one of the island's diverse microclimates. Whether it is thriving in montane cloud forest atop the towering Mount Kinabalu (Borneo's tallest mountain) or fighting for light in thick rainforest - where a plant could adapt to exploit a location it has.

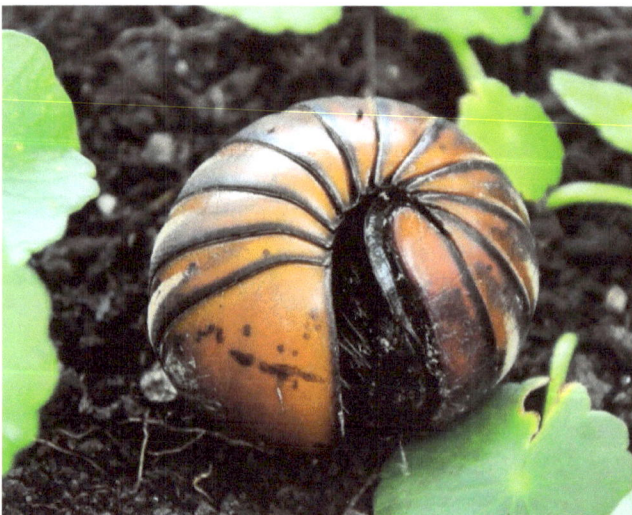
Giant pill millipede (*Bothrobelum rugosum*)

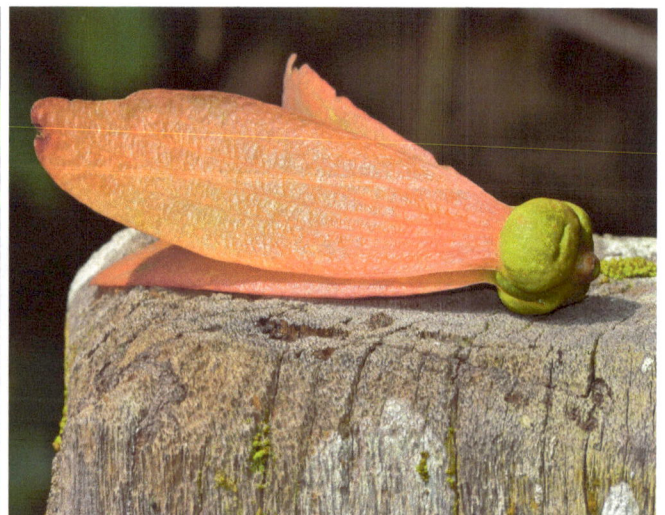
Winged fruit of the Dipterocarpaceae family

Mt Kinabalu is the highest mountain in Borneo

An environmental house of cards

Dipterocarp forests are areas dominated by the giant trees of the Dipterocarpaceae family. This family is united by an unusual winged fruit that can travel great distances when falling from the tall trees. These forests carpet the lowlands of Borneo and are havens of speciation. As many as two hundred different tree species have been recorded within only one hectare of forest, and just one of the enormous dipterocarp trees may house up to ten thousand different invertebrate species. Over two hundred and seventy species of dipterocarp trees have been identified in Borneo, most of which occur nowhere else in the world.

Wetland in Sabah, Borneo

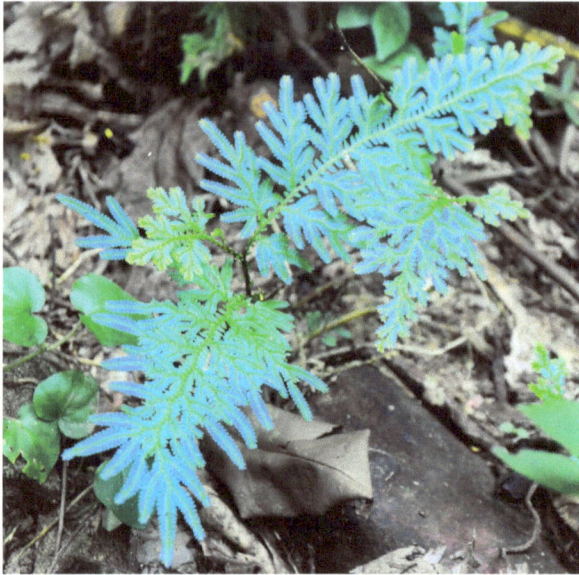

Blue peacock spike moss (*Selaginella willdenowii*)

Another uniting characteristic of the dipterocarp family lies in their rare and irregular flowering cycles. Flowering events only occur once or twice every decade. They are thought to be triggered by a natural climatic event known as the El Niño Southern Oscillation. Due to this climatic activation, dipterocarp flowering occurrences are synchronised over extensive areas. This reliance on climate events for reproduction could have easily inhibited the dipterocarps' likelihood of becoming vegetation of any sort of dominance. Still, the family can be found far and wide on Borneo.

Clever adaptations to fill challenging niches

While dipterocarps dominate the forest canopy and receive light in abundance, life can be more challenging on the forest floor. Some plants have adapted perfectly to the low light and shaded conditions, but what happens when the canopy above sways in the wind and intense sunshine penetrates the understory? It can damage shade-loving plants when prolonged or occurring too frequently, but the electric blue peacock spike moss (*Selaginella willdenowii*) has developed a defence for such occurrences. A thin layer of cells produces the blue iridescence of the beautifully eye-catching species. These cells appear in the upper cuticle of leaves and form reflective surfaces that increase the plants' ability to deflect excessive light.

The forest floor can also be exceptionally moist, particularly in Borneo's prevalent peat swamp forests. These forests occur when anaerobic and waterlogged soil prevents the decomposition of organic matter. Over time a thick layer of partially decomposed and acidic 'peat' is formed, and to survive in these niche environments, plants have needed to evolve different adaptations entirely.

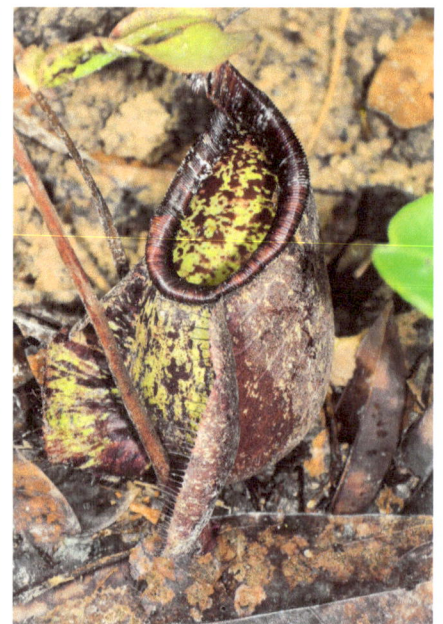

Pitcher plants of the *Nepenthes* genus on display at Bogor Botanic Gardens

An adaptation favoured by many plants growing in poor waterlogged soils (or without soil altogether) is to secure nutrients with specialised organs above ground rather than using their roots. This trait is perhaps best represented by Borneo's pitcher plants (*Nepenthes* spp.) which have become almost synonymous with the island due to their prevalence. Pitcher plants are so named because they have evolved pitcher-shaped leaves that form pitfall traps. These traps can obtain valuable nutrients by capturing and digesting insects and small animals.

More recently, it has been discovered that some pitcher plants prefer a more mutualistic arrangement with animals rather than a fatal one. The pitcher plant *Nepenthes hemsleyana* grows in the peat forests of Borneo and is a common roost for a small mammal known as the Hardwicke's woolly bat (*Kerivoula hardwickii*). In return for its perch, the bat deposits nitrogen-rich faeces directly into the pitchers of *N. hemsleyana*, resulting in a benefit for all. Other *Nepenthes* species offer a nectar-like reward atop their pitchers. It is thought the substance

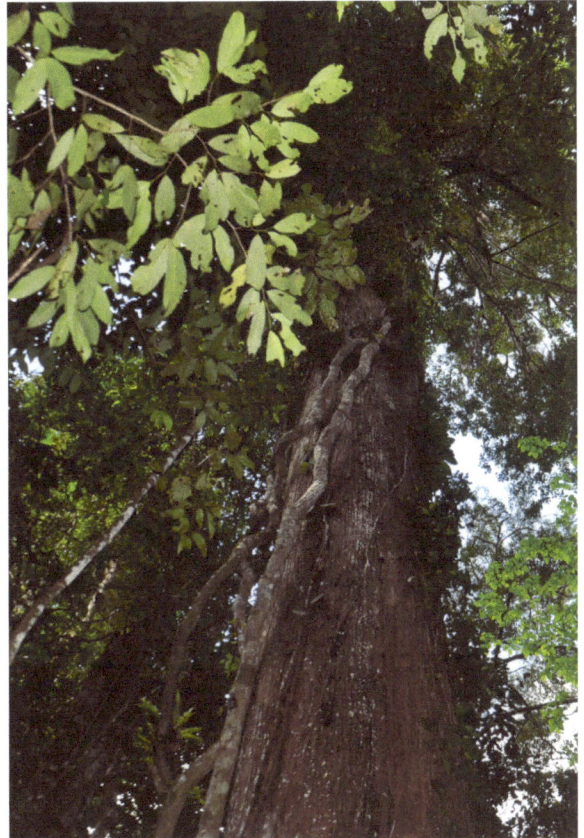

Tetrastigma tuberculatum vine

has a laxative effect, ensuring no visiting animal leaves without making a deposit for the plants. Whatever their form or function, the evolution of the pitcher has resulted in a highly successful group of plants.

Developing bud of *Rafflesia pricei*

Flower development of *Rafflesia patma*   Bud opening to reveal fleshy petals   Open flowers will last just a few days

From invisible to enormous

Though pitcher plants are widespread throughout Borneo, the island is best known for another plant. A plant that progressed down a different evolutionary path allowing it to achieve the illustrious title of the world's largest flower. The corpse flower (*Rafflesia arnoldii*) earned its common name because of the foul odour of rotting meat the flower emits to attract carrion-feeding pollinators. Its fleshy red mass grows up to a metre in width, so the flower could quite literally be mistaken for a corpse.

Happening upon a rafflesia flower among the moist leaf litter of Southeast Asia's rainforests, it's almost as though something somewhere went awry, way back along the tree of life. The plant is entirely parasitic, void of any leaves or stems, and exists entirely within the tissues of its host until it is ready to reproduce. Highly specialised, members of the genus rely wholly on a specific genus of vines (*Tetrastigma* spp.) to act as hosts and supply their nutrient and water needs. Due to this parasitic nature, rafflesias have long discarded a need to photosynthesise, and one species from the Philippines, *Rafflesia lagascae*, appears to have evolved without the chloroplast genome altogether.

Rafflesia pricei in bloom

Members of the *Tetrastigma* genus, while not parasitic, are opportunistic themselves and often survive at the expense of other plants. They are 'lianas', long-stemmed, woody vines which root in the soil at ground level before using other plants as supports to climb toward the forest canopy in search of direct sunlight. Plants like *Rafflesia* spp. and *Tetrastigma* spp. highlight the fact that there is an undeniable case of plants besting plants, driving tropical island speciation across Southeast Asia, Borneo, and around the world.

Many *Rafflesia* species are highly selective when it comes to which *Tetrastigma* species they will parasitise. *Rafflesia arnoldii* prefers *T. leucostaphylum*, while *T. tuberculatum* attracts several species of *Rafflesia*. With this selectivity in mind, *Rafflesia* species work within a minute window of opportunity to achieve germination. Seeds must be deposited near just the right species of vine. This dispersal may be aided by small mammals that eat the fleshy fruit of the plants

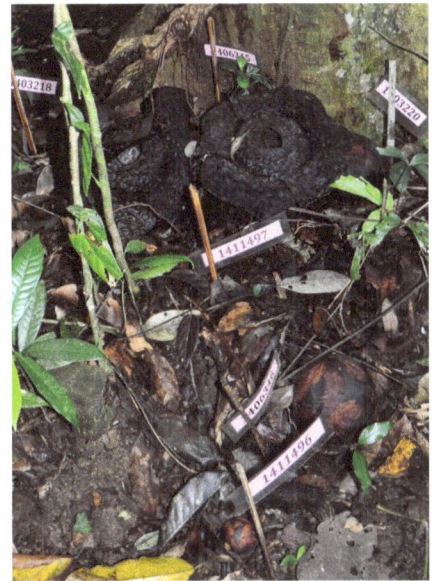

Population of *Rafflesia pricei* being catalogued

and ants attracted to a small protein-rich attachment on its seeds known as an elaiosome. Even with the assistance of these seed dispersal agents, the successful germination of a rafflesia plant is a miraculous feat against all odds.

Nevertheless, a lucky minority of seeds are deposited near a suitable host. When this occurs, the plants will germinate and enter the tissues of the tetrastigma vines using modified parasitic roots known as haustoria. Once the plants have successfully colonised their hosts, they remain unseen, stealing food and water until they have accumulated enough stored supplies to attempt to produce the energy-intensive flowers for which they are known. The production of rafflesia flowers is not a quick process, and several of the species produce blooms that take many months to reach maturity. Beginning first as a small

Ranger shows caterpillar damage on bud of *Rafflesia pricei*

Tetrasigma vine parasitised by *Rafflesia patma* being grafted on to a new host

swollen growth in the dermal tissue of the host, the buds grow to resemble something like a fleshy cabbage before finally opening to full bloom. Amazingly, after months of development, these flowers are only open for a few days before shrivelling into decay.

Like seed dispersal, the budding stage of its lifecycle is a precarious time for the *Rafflesia* genus. It is the first time the plants visibly hint of their existence and requiring several months to develop; they emerge defenceless against predation. The growing flowers are a favourite of caterpillars and many hungry insects thriving in the tropical rainforest. As a result, bud mortality is high, and only a small portion of the flowers survive to reach maturity. The genus is facing more significant threats in recent years, as deforestation occurs across Borneo and Southeast Asia at an increasing rate. Once covering approximately seventy-five percent of its landmass, Borneo's forest cover has now dwindled to just fifty percent, as logging and land clearance to make way for palm oil plantations wreaks havoc on the natural environment.

Hope in an uphill battle

Covering more than three hundred and fifty hectares of the Tambunan district in Borneo, the Rafflesia Forest Reserve was established to reduce the effect of environmental degradation on the genus and protect the abundant rafflesia plants in the area. In the reserve, rafflesia populations, particularly *R. pricei*, are carefully monitored, documented, and studied. *R. pricei* is one of the prettiest species of the genus and does not produce the foul odour of many of its cousins. Perhaps owing to this lack of smell and attractive appearance, the Rafflesia Forest Reserve is also important for ecotourism in the area, allowing income to be generated in the absence of logging and palm oil production. Visitors from around the world pursue the reserve for a chance to see the iconic plants in bloom, but the trip can be a gamble. Depending on what is happening within the reserve, visitors may trek for as little as a few minutes, to several hours, to find a colony of rafflesias with an open flower, especially one that hasn't started to discolour and breakdown after its brief window of maturity.

Across the Javan Sea at Indonesia's Bogor Botanic Gardens, staff have been working on more reliable ways to allow visitors a chance to witness the amazing blooms and ensure the conservation of the genus. Here a steady supply of flowers is produced in the domestic location without the need to wager on a chance sighting, and the techniques involved in accomplishing this feat are ingenious. To date, no one has been able to successfully germinate rafflesia seeds and have them colonise a tetrastigma vine in cultivation. Domestic populations are not

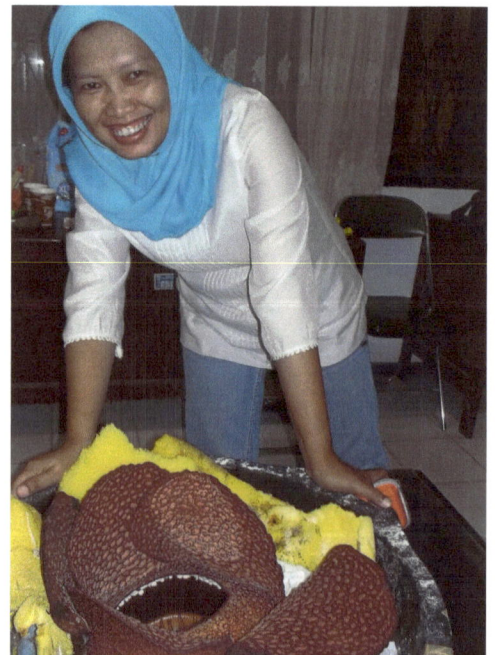

Rafflesia patma being packed for the International Horticulture Goyang

Amorphophallus titanum

Amorphophallus konjac

Amorphophallus maximus

unheard of, but they are usually achieved by transplanting an already parasitised tetrastigma plant. This has been achieved at the Bogor Botanic Gardens; however, behind the scenes, some plants have been produced a little differently.

Grafting is a common method of propagation that consists of implanting the parts of one plant into the tissues of another. At Bogor, it has been discovered that this process is a valuable tool for the ongoing preservation of the *Rafflesia* genus. By grafting portions of *T. scariosum*, known to have been parasitised by *R. patma*, onto an unaffected *T. scariosum*, researchers at the gardens have been able to produce a steady supply of domestic blooms over many years. This success comes at a critical time and offers hope for the survival of this charismatic genus. It also provides hope for a world of plant enthusiasts aspiring to see the flowers up close but who can't make the trip to the tropical rainforests of Southeast Asia. The public appeal of these flowers is immense, and just a single bloom of *Rafflesia patma* raised at Bogor and sent to the International Horticulture Goyang (a flower show held annually in Korea) drew in tens of thousands of viewers throughout the event.

When ensuring the survival of any species, the goal is to preserve genetic diversity, and for plants, this is achieved through sexual propagation. Unless self-fertilised, pollination of flowers results in seeds containing the genetics from two parent plants. Presently the grafting of *R. patma* produces genetic clones of the plants from which the material was taken, so ongoing research into successful seed propagation is invaluable. Unfortunately, pollination and seed production

Amorphophallus paeoniifolius

A single leaf of *A. titanum* can resemble a tree

in cultivated rafflesia plants present challenges of their own. Rafflesia flowers are unisexual, meaning they are either male or female. While there are a disproportionate number of male flowers occurring in the wild, blooms from grafted material have tended to be female. It is a case of botanical irony and as the plants' pollen is only viable for about eight hours, getting wild pollen from the male flowers to the female flowers in cultivation is nearly impossible.

Rafflesia is an elusive and enigmatic genus of plants that appear to survive in their natural environments against all odds. Domestic cultivation has come with similar challenges. Gardening with these tropical giants requires patience, perseverance, and ingenuity, but the Bogor Botanic Gardens staff have got this recipe just right, and the task ahead is in good hands.

Meet the family, excuse the smell

Rafflesias are not the only botanical giants in cultivation at the Bogor Botanic Gardens, nor are they the only 'corpse flowers'. The common name is confusingly shared with another aromatic plant unique to Southeast Asia. *Amorphophallus titanum* was first (and more correctly) named the corpse flower as it was a direct translation from the Indonesian name for the plant. However, both specimens produce a similar smell of rotting meat, so the name corpse flower has become mutually synonymous. *A. titanum* is also known as the titan arum, owing to its enormous size. The flowering structure of some specimens can surpass a gargantuan three metres in height.

While not as large as their enormous cousin, many *Amorphophallus* species occur across Southeast Asia. One species, *A. maximus*, has even been found in the subtropics of Africa. They come in all shapes, sizes, and colours, from the minuscule *A. obscurus* to the bizarrely attractive *A. paeoniifolius*. Some have medicinal value, while others are edible. *A. Konjac* from China is widely cultivated across Asia where it is used to produce a form of flour. It is the main ingredient in shirataki noodles which are hugely popular in Japan and gaining traction as a high fibre, low carb dieting aid in the West. The intriguing genus is part of the arum family (Araceae), and while all *Amorphophallus* species have their merit, none commands attention like the mighty titan arum. It has a Latin name that can make botanists blush, and when a flower emerges, every five to ten years, the plants can draw in a cast of thousands.

A. titanum has a curious lifecycle. From seed, the plants will take many years to mature. They produce an underground energy storage organ known as a tuber, which serves a similar function to a bulb but is physiologically quite different. From this tuber, a single leaf is produced by the plant during most years on its long journey to blooming. Each leaf can last up to eighteen months. During this time,

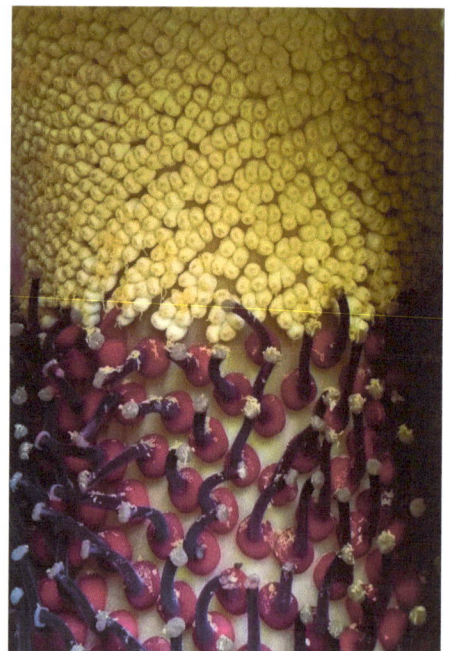

Male flowers of *A. titanum* sit above the females

it will capture and store valuable energy in the plant's underground tuber in preparation for its resource-intensive flowering event. Between each leaf cycle, the plants will die back and enter a period of dormancy. As they reach maturity, the single divided leaf of an *A. titanum* can be so large it resembles a small tree.

Though its flower is much smaller than *A. titanum*, *R. arnoldii* still holds the record as the world's largest flower. This is because the bloom of *A. titanum* is a complex floral structure made up of many smaller individual flowers. In botanical terms, this structure is known as an inflorescence. Inflorescences are seen in different forms across the plant kingdom. So, technically *A. titanum* holds the record for being the world's largest unbranched inflorescence instead.

In members of the arum family, inflorescences are made up of unbranched flowers packed tightly into part of a column known as a spadix. While still developing, the spadix and its vulnerable flowers are protected within a modified leaf known as a spathe. When ripe, this spathe fans out to reveal a brightly coloured landing pad for insects. As the flowers open, the spadix begins to produce heat and the foul smell of rotting meat as a beacon for pollinators. The whole event only lasts about forty-eight hours before the flowers lose viability and the plants begin to produce fruit or recede into dormancy.

The spadices of *Amorphophallus* spp. comprise of both male flowers and female flowers. As pollen-covered insects are funnelled toward the spadix by the plant's spathe, they inevitably bump into

Tuber of *A. titanum*

Tubers of A. *Konjac*

the female flowers, and pollination occurs. However, self-pollination is undesirable, and the plants of this genus have evolved a clever way to avoid it. Female flowers open in the first twenty-four hours of a bloom, while the males remain closed. This is when the flowers are at their most fragrant. The male flowers open and expel pollen the next day, but by then, the female flowers have become unreceptive.

A. titanum being propagated by leaf cuttings

A. titanum can also be propagated using tissue culture

Although both *Rafflesia* and *Amorphophallus* species share a common name in 'corpse flower' and release the smell of rotten meat when flowering, they are entirely unrelated. This is a blessing for horticulturists and researchers working with *Amorphophallus* spp. because, unlike rafflesias, several techniques have been developed to propagate the plants. Seed from many species germinate readily and tubers which can be divided into new plants, eventually multiply underground. However, this is a slow process, and faster tuber production has been achieved using leaf cuttings. The leaves of some *Amorphophallus* spp. can be cut into small segments and set in a propagation medium to produce new plants. Given time, many small tubers will form on the wounded surfaces of the leaf segments, much faster than they would form naturally beneath the soil. Unlike species of *Rafflesia*, *Amorphophallus* spp. have made their way to botanic gardens around the world. While they still face threats within their natural environment, the genus now has a global safety net.

Questions, answers, and moving forward

Borneo is a vast island, so large, it is shared between three countries, Malaysia, Indonesia, and Brunei. The island is home to its share of *Amorphophallus* species, but *A. titanum* is not one of them and can only be found naturally on the Indonesian island of Sumatra. *R. arnoldii* is reported to occur on both islands but no others. Other species of plants appear to endure broadly across the Southeast Asian islands. Some

A titan arum flowering at the New York Botanic Gardens

have likely been introduced, but the dispersal of others may be linked to an ancient land bridge known as the Sundaic Region, thought to have linked the Malay Archipelago several million years ago. Knowing there was such a dramatic geographical change in this region provides more questions than it does answers as to why the plants and animals found on the islands today are dispersed in the way they are. What did the common ancestors of today's species look like before the landmass was divided by rising seas and islands drove speciation? What led species to survive on one island but become extinct on another? Why have some islands diversified in species from a common ancestor faster than others?

With new species still being discovered on Borneo and across the region, we may never have all the pieces to solves these puzzles but preserving and studying what has already been found is a good start. The propagators and researchers working behind the scenes at Bogor Botanic Gardens and botanical gardens worldwide are not often thought of as gardeners in a conventional sense. Still, in an era of rapid and extensive environmental change, perhaps plant preservation is the most valuable and rewarding form of gardening there is?

Gardens of Innovation and Respite
Jerusalem Botanic Gardens
Jerusalem, Israel

A city of significance

Widely regarded as one of the holiest places on Earth, Jerusalem is a location held sacred in the hearts of many around the world. Thought to be one of the oldest cities on the planet, Jerusalem possesses sites of significance for all three of the major Abrahamic faiths, Islam, Judaism, and Christianity. For Christians, the Church of the Holy Sepulchre is thought to be the site of the crucifixion, burial, and resurrection of Jesus. There is nowhere more sacred in Judaism than Jerusalem's Western Wall and the Temple Mount, which it borders. While for the Islamic faith, the Al-Aqsa Mosque and the nearby Dome of the Rock are some of the religion's most important locations.

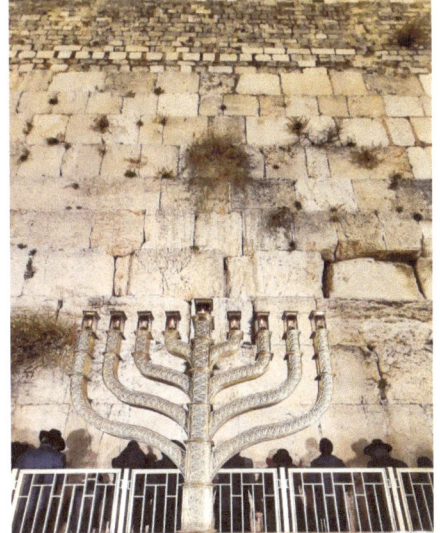

Jewish men praying at the Western Wall

However, amidst the ancient buildings of Jerusalem's Old City region, it quickly becomes apparent that the area is significant for many lesser-known denominations. Cathedrals, monasteries, mosques, and synagogues stand side by side. Russian and Greek Orthodox neighbour German Lutherans, while the Syriac Church practices the earliest known form of Christian liturgy. Even the World Centre of the Bahai faith, while not in Jerusalem, stands in nearby Haifa. Considering its age and the prevalence of religious significance in Israel, it is no wonder the area has been one of the most contested portions of land on Earth over the millennia.

The Dome of the Rock stands out in the landscape of Jerusalem

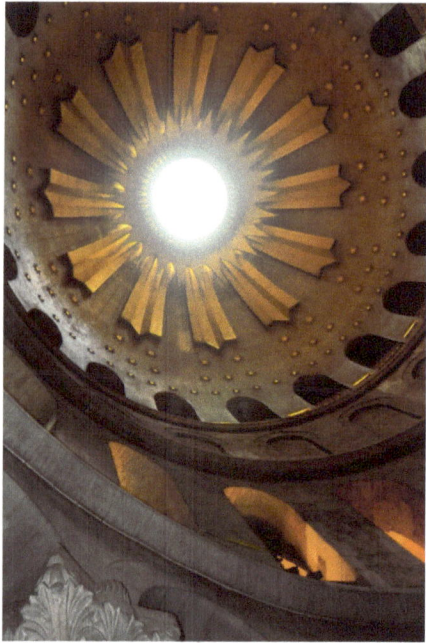

Ornate ceiling of the Church of the Holy Sepulchre

It is an unfortunate reality that the region which is modern-day Israel, is somewhat synonymous with dispute. However, long before arriving at its most recent state, the land bore witness to conflicts over hundreds and even thousands of years. In centuries gone, it has been ruled by empires from the Babylonians, Persians, and Romans to the Egyptians, Ottomans, and British, in addition to many others. Each empire leaving a cultural mark on the landscape. It is a contentious history for such a small piece of Earth, as Israel measures just over four hundred kilometres in length and a mere one hundred and thirty-five kilometres across at its widest point.

At its heart lies Jerusalem, a city preserved in time, maintaining its ancient appearance in a modern era. This is due primarily to the city's municipal laws, which require that all buildings are faced with local Jerusalem stone. The sedimentary material found in hues of cream to pink and yellow has been used for construction for centuries. Originating early in the twentieth century, the mandate to ensure all buildings, old or new, maintain at least a façade made of the material contributes enormously to the charm of the landscape. In a world where cities are increasingly littered with billboards and neon lights, Jerusalem remains unbusied by paint and excess colour. With its pale palette shining in the Mediterranean sun, the city has an appearance fitting its significance.

Though Israel is a small country, it possesses a remarkable diversity in terrain and climate. Broadly, the region's Mediterranean climate produces long hot summers and short cold, wet winters, but Israel is also a land of environmental contrast. Regional conditions vary considerably. Almost half of the country is regarded as desert, and areas in the south receive very little rainfall. The coastal plains along the Mediterranean Sea remain humid and near tropical in summer, while the high country in the north is

The Georgian Monastery of the Cross, one of Jerusalem's many significant religious sites

OFF THE GARDEN PATH

lush and green, producing rainfall in abundance. This diversity in environments has fostered the emergence of an equally diverse array of plants, and Israel is home to over two thousand native species, of which close to three hundred are endemic and occur naturally nowhere else.

Far from barren

For some, the Middle East conjures up images of dusty barren deserts, but in Israel, the warmth of spring brings with it the emergence of a mass of brightly coloured blooms anywhere there is moisture in the soil and in some cases, even where there isn't. Geophytes are perennial plants that spend a portion of their life in dormancy, retaining valuable food and water in underground storage organs for growth when conditions are right. The arid deserts in some parts of Israel have proven perfect locations for the evolution of geophytes which make up an impressive eleven percent of the country's native species.

Short-lived ephemerals handle the dry conditions in another way. This type of plant can survive in the driest of conditions for many years as a seed. Then, when precipitation does arrive,

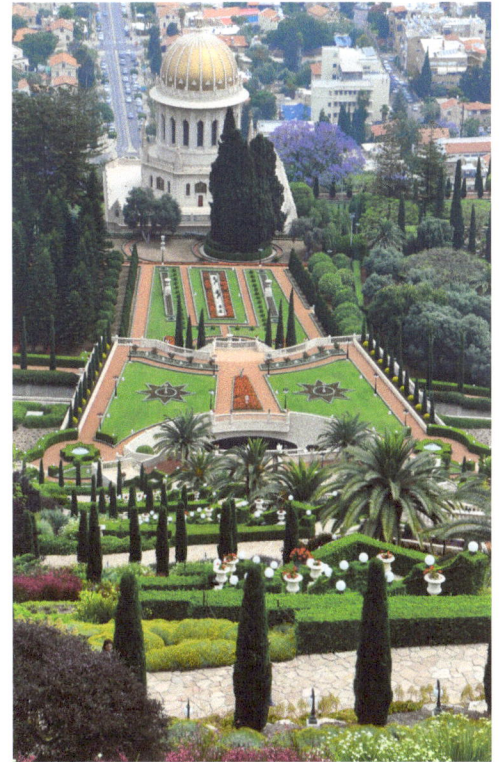

Gardens at the World Centre of the Bahai faith

the plants spring into life. Utilising a specialised and efficient metabolism, they grow, flower, fruit, and set seed in just a few weeks, while there is still moisture in the soil. This may occur several times in favourable years, and the plants might not be seen again for many years in between. The seeds of short-lived ephemerals employ various strategies to ensure they do not germinate prematurely, without an adequate rain event. Some contain chemicals that inhibit germination and require significant amounts

Jerusalem bell flower (*Campanula hierosolymitana*)

Desert broomrape *(Cistanche tubulosa)*

of water to be removed, while others have thick seed coats that require extended periods of weathering.

Broomrapes are another group of plants common to Israel that spend much of their lives unseen and below ground but in a more sinister fashion than conventional geophytes. These plants are holoparasitic and need to rely entirely on a host to provide the energy gained through photosynthesis. While broomrapes produce roots, much of their water and nutrient is supplemented by the extensive root systems of their much larger hosts. The parasitic nature of the plants, which are members of the Orobanchaceae family, has allowed them to spread far and wide, becoming serious pests in some parts of the world. However, in other regions, they are prized. For example, the desert broomrapes *Cistanche tubulosa* and *Cistanche deserticola* are important in traditional Chinese medicine, while the common broomrape *Orobanche minor* has a long history in Western folk medicine.

Many economically damaging broomrapes reduce agricultural crop yields and contribute to harvesting issues, but some are also rare and even endangered due to habitat destruction. *Cistanche fissa* is known to occur widely in the Middle East but was only recently observed in Israel for the first time after heavy rain and a year of ideal environmental conditions allowed the species to bloom. The fleeting nature of geophytes and ephemerals means they are sometimes

Orobanche sp. in the north of Israel

OFF THE GARDEN PATH

Iris atrofusca

Tulipa agenensis

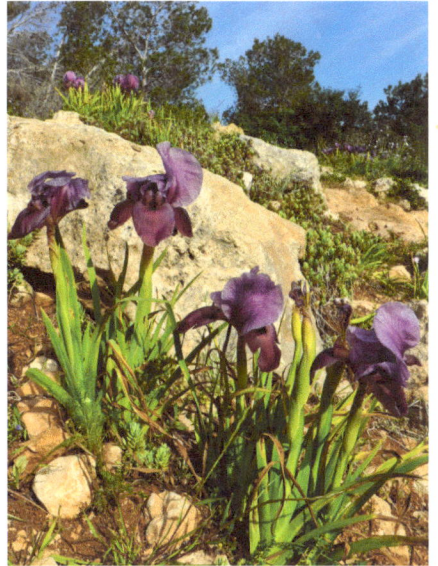

Iris haynei

difficult to observe, and this offers the slim but tantalising possibility that anyone could discover an elusive species, new to science, when in the right place at the right time.

Growing alongside the unusual broomrapes, some of Israel's endemic plant species are far easier to recognise, as their cousins have been commercialised and can be found in gardens the world over. The region offers native poppies, irises, anemones, and tulips, among many others, but most have experienced limited commercialisation. The four species of tulip native to the region (*Tulipa agenensis*, *T. systola*, *T. biflora*, and *T. lownei*) have more delicate flowers than their domesticated relatives but are no less special.

Sea daffodil (*Pancratium maritimum*)

Rare Jericho garlic (*Allium hierochuntinum*)

Botanical colour in spring

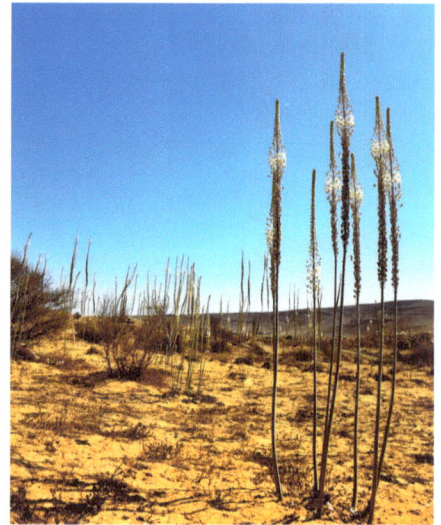

Sea squill (*Drimia maritima*)

The same cannot be said for Israel's native irises, which are just as impressive as many garden varieties, if not more so. The Nazareth iris (*Iris bismarckiana*) commands attention with light violet blooms covered with large dark spots. In contrast, the Gilead iris (*I. atrofusca*) presents strikingly dark brown or even black flowers. Not to be outdone, the Gilboa iris (*I. haynei*) displays purple flowers covered in a dense network of veins interspersed with delicate dots of darker pigment. Displaying far more than native irises the Mediterranean becomes a botanical playground in spring. It is an ideal time for plant enthusiasts to visit to see geophytes at their best, although there are also good floral displays in autumn.

Israel's oldest *Ziziphus spina-christi* thought to be close to two thousand years old

History locked in aging relics

Israel is also home to a range of native trees and reflective of the region's age; many are of historical religious significance. For example, the medicinally valuable Christ's thorn jujube (*Ziziphus spina-christi*) is a long-lived tree of the area. The oldest specimen found in the country is thought to be up to two thousand years old. Its edible fruit is an important food source for wild animals, and its flowers provide forage for bees, but *Z. spina-christi* is significant for another reason. It is thought by many that it was the thorny stems of this species that were used to make the crown of thorns Jesus was forced to wear when crucified. However, other theories suggest the crown was forged from a plant far more brutal - an acacia.

Due to taxonomical changes over the years, acacia is a common name used for a variety of visually similar genera. It was once a widespread recognised genus, but after a controversial decision early in the century, now true *Acacia* spp. are only found in Australia. The acacias of Africa and the Middle East have all been allocated new botanical names, but the common name acacia is still in use. The acacias of Africa and the Middle East are an intriguing group, having developed some amazing defence mechanisms against predation over the years. Some are thought to be capable of releasing chemical signals when eaten by browsing herbivores, triggering nearby plants to produce toxic substances in their tissues, which can kill the animals if they continue to feed in the area. Other acacias form mutualistic relationships with aggressive ants for defence against

Vachellia tortilis subsp. *raddiana*

Ancient olive (*Olea europaea*)

A takeover by giant animatronic dinosaurs has been one of many special events held at the gardens

View inside the Jerusalem Botanic Gardens' tropical conservatory

grazing. The twisted acacia (*Vachellia tortilis* subsp. *raddiana*) employs a different defence. When eaten, the plant responds by growing larger and larger thorns. Reaching several centimetres in length, a crown of thorns made from this species would have been a truly horrific creation.

Along with *Z. spina-christi*, the region is home to another tree species capable of reaching a remarkable age. The humble olive (*Olea europaea*) can live for several thousands of years. A staple ingredient on any dinner table across the Mediterranean, the trees are an easily overlooked part of the landscape, but ancient specimens in Israel have recently revealed a long-forgotten secret. Genetic testing on a population thought to be over one thousand years old has shown that the above-ground parts of the plants are genetically different from those of the root zone. The findings reveal that humans have been utilising the sophisticated horticultural practice of grafting for thousands of years.

A garden of many functions

Like many countries around the world, Israel is facing challenges posed by climate variability and environmental extremes. With so many wonderful species found in the country and neighbouring regions, the importance of protecting as many plants as possible is well recognised. Israel has an international reputation as a centre of innovation, and the efforts for plant preservation undertaken in this part of the world are no exception.

Perched on a hilly slope in the neighbourhood of Neyot stand the Jerusalem Botanic Gardens, where much of the research into the conservation of the nation's plants occurs. Spanning over thirty acres and home to the most extensive plant collection in the Middle East, the value of this facility is complemented by the adjoining Givat Ram Campus of the Hebrew University and its significant herbarium collection. The Jerusalem Botanic Gardens maintains a living collection of over six thousand plant species from across the world, displayed throughout the grounds according to their geographical origins, but the conservation efforts for these plants start well before they are put out on display.

One aspect that makes the gardens so innovative is the international collaboration involved in many of its projects. Aided by a thriving volunteer community, the Jerusalem Botanic Gardens engage in the exchange of rare seed and plant material globally with numerous centres of botanical excellence abroad. The gardens also host horticultural scholars from around the world who undertake placements at the site, bringing with them knowledge and international experience in plant preservation.

Whether involving volunteers, permanent staff, students, or scholars, the first step on the journey of Israel's threatened plants is their initial discovery and the subsequent retrieval of propagation material. Many threatened and endangered plant species in the country are protected by law and can only be collected under

The conservatory nearing the end of its recent construction

a special licence held by the Jerusalem Botanic Gardens. Once approved, the plant material is taken to the gardens, where the specimens are propagated, fostered, and raised in the hope that they will eventually provide seed themselves. These programs have been so successful in some cases that the seeds of several rare plants have been released commercially for members of the public to grow in home gardens.

The gardens are separated into phytogeographical sections suited to the climate in Jerusalem and include areas dedicated to Southern Africa, Europe, North America, Australia, Southwest and Central Asia, and the Mediterranean. However, to ensure the location can display a diverse array of species, the Jerusalem Botanic Gardens also feature a tropical conservatory. Possessing a unique design, the conservatory was built into the surrounding bedrock, which provides visitors with an enchantingly immersive experience.

Studies in hydroponic farming provide an alternative for youth who have struggled with traditional schooling

Complemented by running water, vertical gardens, and the extensive use of vines that scramble over any surface they touch, the conservatory transports visitors from the Middle East to a tropical paradise.

It is not just through the conservation of plants that the Jerusalem Botanic Gardens demonstrate innovation. Perhaps the most apparent difference between these gardens and others worldwide is their extensive emphasis on education and community participation. The inclusive site incorporates excellent interpretive signage and educational infrastructure for children. Regular guided tours are offered, and there is even a train to help transport those with limited mobility around the large site. In addition, the gardens have hosted various international events over the years to build awareness of the environment and encourage people to engage with nature. From light shows and art exhibitions to being overtaken by giant animatronic dinosaurs, it is never long between new and exciting attractions. Though several large events are held each year, the smaller ongoing programs have the most significance for the community.

The progressive activities offered at the Jerusalem Botanic Gardens are made possible by the gardens' diverse partnerships with community stakeholders. Many varied and innovative horticultural programs have come to pass due to active collaborations between organisations from schools and farms to a global network of botanic gardens. A recent example has been the establishment of a substantial hydroponic farm at the site, which allows adolescents who have struggled in traditional schooling, the opportunity to gain new skills in the increasingly important industry for food security. Work placement possibilities have even been established in conjunction with the country's correctional system and as a substitute for military service. These programs are accompanied by many more and often utilise the practice of horticultural therapy.

Horticultural therapy is the process by which gardening, and plants can be used to improve an individual's physical or mental well-being. Whether to assist in reducing stress, depression, and other mental health conditions or support recovery after surgery and trauma, horticultural therapy presents a valuable aid in treatment. When the sun is shining, it provides a boost in vitamin D while outside, and some studies indicate that a common soil bacterium (*Mycobacterium vaccae*) may encourage serotonin

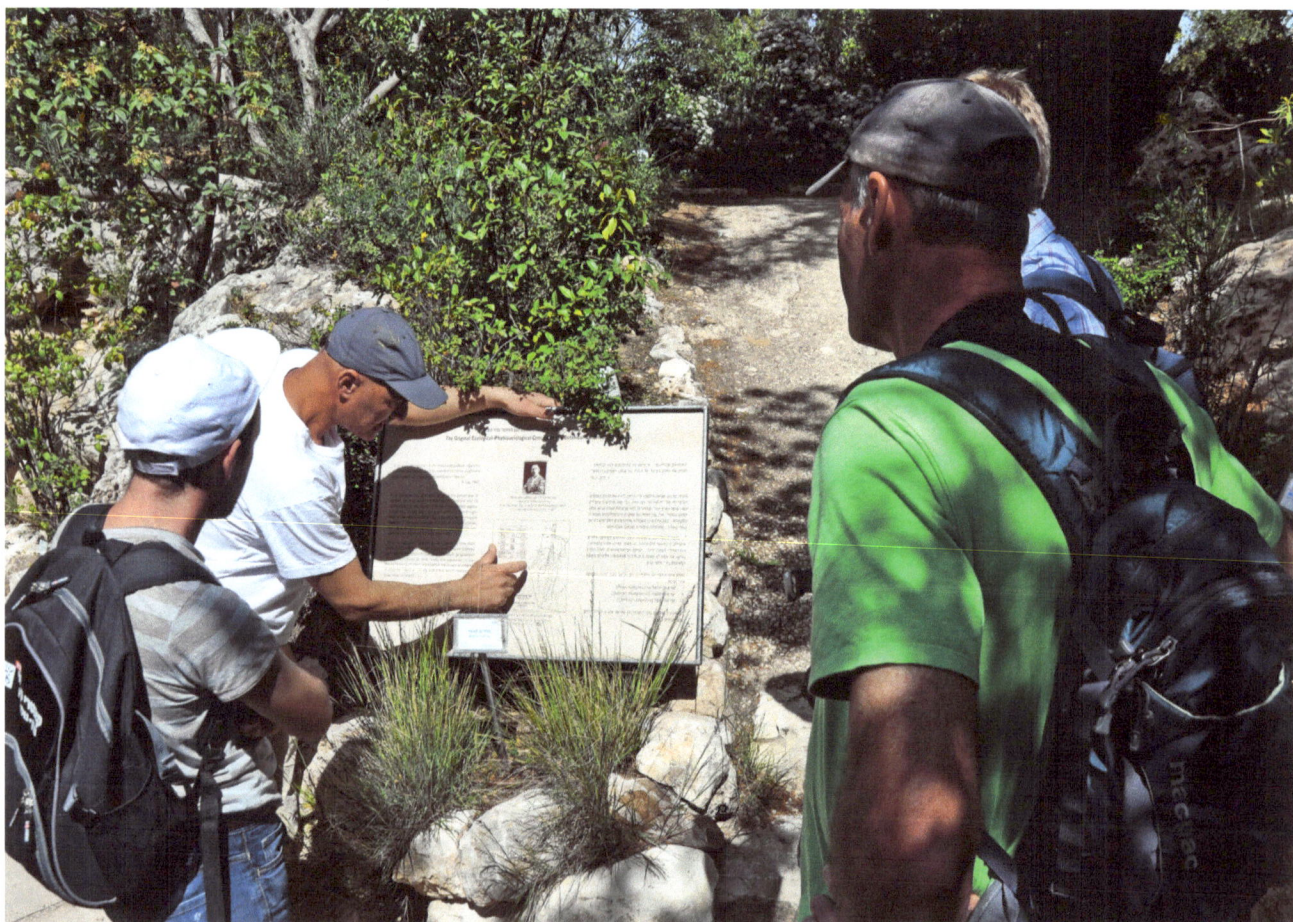

A gardener explains some of the site's excellent interpretive signage

production and function as a natural antidepressant. In addition, gardening helps improve motor skills, and being amongst nature has a general calming effect; in short, plants and gardening make us feel good.

Horticultural therapy is something that the Jerusalem Botanic Gardens facilitates very effectively. To be able to care for and look after another living thing can be an empowering experience. By tending to plants, people receive an increased sense of responsibility and purpose. Volunteering and gardening are also very social activities and can reduce feelings of isolation. Add to these benefits healthy and localised food production or the conservation of rare species and the benefits of the community programs the Jerusalem Botanic Gardens facilitate start to add up.

In the sometimes-turbulent Middle East, gardens offer a politically neutral opportunity for respite and recovery from the surrounding environment. In Israel, there are no gardens more effective in this regard than the Jerusalem Botanic Gardens. Gardens that opened their gates to the public in the mid-eighties and have since gone from strength to strength; gardens that manage to innovatively combine science, conservation, education, and community in engaging programs that benefit participants and the environment.

These gardens play a pivotal role in fostering the well-being of the region's plants and people, and for all the historical wonders to be encountered in Jerusalem, it has to be said that the true wonder in the ancient city is a more recent and green one.

Lotuses in bloom on Jerusalem Botanic Gardens' feature lake

Gardening for Survival
Subsistence Farmers in Ultimate Isolation
Kigoma region, Tanzania

A nation of secluded diversity

When descending into Africa and the depths of the tropical savannah, it isn't likely that any anticipation of an elegantly maintained garden setting will be met with much satisfaction. A seemingly endless sea of green from above and virtually impenetrable from the ground, the landscape is as wild as any could be. Yet, as harsh as the conditions may seem, gardening is certainly still practiced here. In fact, the skills of a gardener are all the more valued in this part of the world. In lands so inhospitable, gardening is not just a pastime; it becomes a necessity.

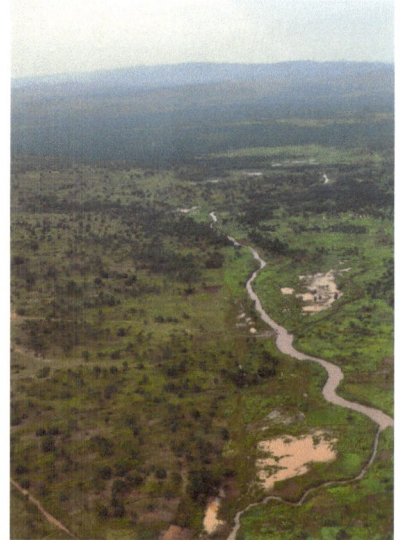

Tanzanian tropical savannah

Consisting of over fifty countries, Africa is an expansive continent and thought to be home to three thousand different tribal groups. The East African nation of Tanzania maintains this diversity. It plays host to well over one hundred of these groups, from the Hadza people in the north, who are considered one of the last hunter-gatherer tribes in Africa, to the distinctive Maasai warrior tribes, world-renowned for their unique culture and brightly coloured attire. Lesser known abroad are a further mix of ethnic groups united by the Bantu language, which extends across Africa and who account for the majority of Tanzania's population.

Kigoma region, Tanzania

OFF THE GARDEN PATH

This diversity in culture makes for a fascinating plethora of cuisine and agricultural practices to match. Arguably void of gardeners, the Hadza maintain an age-old hunter-gatherer lifestyle, surviving only on what is caught or collected shortly before it is consumed, while many tribes, including the Maasai, are traditionally nomadic pastoralists. The Maasai astonishingly lived on merely the meat, milk, and blood of their cattle in the past. However, in a world increasingly influenced by the west, even these groups are becoming reliant on cultivated crops. The remaining majority of Tanzania's rural inhabitants are relatively sedentary, scattered across the land in isolation, and vulnerable to the elements. For these people, gardening is essential for survival.

Village life in the Kigoma region of Tanzania is basic and challenging but judging by the smiles on people's faces, there is something to be said for the simple life. Families are large and homes modest, often constructed with thatch walls and timber cut from the surrounding forests or using mudbricks finished with grass or palm frond roofs. The staple ingredients consumed are also humble, but with the addition of some local delicacies, including dried fish, they are prepared into meals that are flavoursome, homely, and nourishing.

Group of Maasai men

Woman selling dried fish

Many hands make light work, large families are common in rural Tanzania

Mud huts and cassava plantation

From traditions to diet, plants play their part

The term delicacy might be a little creative when describing some of the other ingredients found in the area. Still, there is no shortage of unusual edible plants to experience in the tropical savannah. Occurring naturally among the dominant grasses and tangled jungle, some species are quite delicate and challenging to find. In contrast, others are naturalised, and invasive, so widespread they are hard to miss.

Without much searching, native *Vigna* species can be found. Their twining stems and distinctive pea flowers contrasting against the green of the surrounding blades of grass they cling to in a desperate search for light. Related to several domesticated bean varieties, many of Tanzania's *Vigna* species have edible fruit. Some species, including *Vigna frutescens*, also possess sweet edible tubers that are a favourite of the Hadza people.

Several members of the spiderwort family (Commelinaceae) are naturalised in Tanzania and have long been adopted by the local groups. The hairy day flower (*Commelina benghalensis*) is one such species, quickly blanketing any bare earth on which a seed may fall and sprawling over surrounding vegetation. However, looking past its weediness *C. benghalensis* is incredibly advantageous to many people across Africa. The leaves and stems can be cooked as a vegetable, particularly in times of food scarcity, and it provides good feed for livestock. Used medicinally, the mucilaginous plant aids in the treatment of boils, ulcers, stomach irritations and, in some tribes, is also thought to combat infertility.

Intriguingly, this plant's value rests not only in food or medicine. For the Maasai, *C. benghalensis* is also culturally significant. It is traditionally used when there is an argument between two people. If either person wants to end the conflict, they can present a portion of *C. benghalensis* as a peace offering of sorts, which effectively puts an end to the issue in the eyes of the tribe and, importantly, its elders. This gesture is taken very seriously by the Maasai. If the dispute is reignited after this point, the individuals will likely face severe punishments set out in tribal law. Far from as common and inconsequential as it first appears, *C. benghalensis* is even used when blessing the cattle that are of such importance to the Maasai's survival.

Endemic to Africa, the herbaceous twiners in the *Cyphia* genus are charming plants that yield flowers quite unlike anything abroad. However, while they might be attractive to look at, it is their edible underground tubers that are the reason they are sought out in many areas. Also occurring at ground level are the strange blooms of an unusual and bizarrely beautiful plant used for everything from treating various ailments to serving as a flavouring condiment in everyday meals. In some areas, it is even considered as an aphrodisiac.

Thonningia sanguinea is the only species in a monotypic genus - there is nothing else quite like it. Roughly translated, a local name for the plant is 'crown of the ground', and when happening upon the flowers, it is quickly apparent the name is fitting. The blooms of *T. sanguinea* are one of the only features that reveal its existence, as the plant is entirely parasitic and spends the majority of its life underground. After germinating, this botanical opportunist attaches itself to a range of host plants from which it will draw nutrients for the remainder of its life. As such, the plant has completely discarded any need for chlorophyll or photosynthesis. It is only when ready to reproduce that *T. sanguinea* develops flowers that emerge through the soil surface wrapped in bright red scale-like leaves, which open to reveal a clustered inflorescence reminiscent of a tiny cauliflower.

In a biological twist, though *T. sanguinea* spends its life as a parasite, surviving at the expense of its hosts, it is uncharacteristically generous when it comes to its pollinators. Both ants and flies visit the flowers for a nectar-rich reward, but it is the muscid flies that also lay their eggs on the flowers that really capitalise on the blooms. After the flowers are pollinated and have produced seed, the hatching larvae of the flies feed on the decaying plant tissues of the flowers, in what is a fantastic display of ecological mutualism.

T. sanguinea is not the only plant in this part of the world that is the solitary species of its genus. When first witnessing the sausage tree (*Kigelia africana*), it is not hard to see why botanists have decided it also lacks any close relatives. Producing hard woody fruits that can reach nearly a metre in length and resemble

Vigna sp.

Cyphia sp.

Commelina benghalensis

Thonningia sanguinea

Fruit of the sausage tree *(Kigelia africana)*

giant sausages suspended in the tree's canopy, this plant is one of a kind. Its fresh fruit is regarded as toxic, though it is an essential ingredient in the fermentation process for the traditional beer of many tribes and its proclaimed medicinal uses are numerous. Once removed from the inedible fruit, the large seeds are also comestible when roasted and often relied upon in times of famine. Far from just a curiosity of folk medicine *K. Africana* has been the subject of much research. Poultices utilising the plant have been used traditionally for centuries, but thanks to recent findings, the species is now used in commercial medicines to treat various dermal conditions, including skin cancer.

Unfortunately, though abundant in botanical wonders, Tanzania is witnessing an ethnobotanical paradox. Because wild medicinal plants are regarded as far more potent than those in cultivation, their collection and sale are leading to many species dwindling in numbers and their survival becoming severely threatened. At the same time, with encroaching Western influence, many tribes are losing the knowledge of traditional medicine handed down and utilised by the generations before them. While wild plant populations are declining, so is their demand.

Cultures worth keeping

In rural Tanzania, whatever can be eaten, will be. And why not? 'Waste not, want not' is a perfect mantra for life in this isolated part of the world. Unfortunately, incidental herbs and plants that are labour intensive to prepare don't make very economical energy sources. So, many cultures throughout Tanzania have come to rely on just a handful of dependable crops for basic sustenance.

Across the world, it is grain crops that account for nearly half of the calories consumed in the daily diet of most humans and form the staple ingredients in the dishes of almost every culture on Earth. However, while high in carbohydrates,

Cassava and beans in the process of being dried

grains often lack many of the essential proteins needed to maintain human health. For these nutrients, grain dishes are usually combined with whatever protein sources are easily accessible. These sources are often legumes or animal products, and it is no accident that iconic dishes from around the world have adhered to this nutritionally balanced formula for thousands of years. From tofu or lentils served with rice in Asia to hummus and pita in the Middle East, even the bean and corn dishes of the Americas repeat this basic pattern.

The villages of the Kigoma region rely on several crops, including 'maharage' (the beans of *Phaseolus vulgaris* varieties), maize (*Zea mays*), and carbohydrate-rich tuberous alternatives to grains, including sweet potatoes (*Ipomoea batatas*) and cassava (*Manihot esculenta*). While sweet potatoes have become popular worldwide and can be seen in markets across the globe, cassava has been less adopted. However, it is still hugely popular in tropical nations where the woody shrub is grown as an annual root crop. High-yielding, cassava provides a much sought-after food source in developing countries. Its drought tolerance and ability to survive in nutrient-poor soils present valuable traits for farmers. When comparing the time and land area required to harvest a consumable product, cassava also delivers far greater calorific production than most grain crops, including rice, wheat, and maize.

Although cassava contains cyanide and all parts of the plant are poisonous when not prepared correctly, both the leaves and tubers can be eaten after being cooked. Better known globally as tapioca, a nutritious flour can be produced by peeling and drying the tubers. The dried material is then ground into a fine powder used as the key ingredient in various puddings and as a thickening agent.

In Tanzania, the flour is used to create a product known as 'ugali', a doughy porridge of variable consistency. Many ugali recipes also call for maize flour but regardless of the formula, ugali has little taste alone and is best eaten with something more flavoursome. Sometimes considered Tanzania's national dish, 'ugali na maharage ya nazi' is a serving of ugali with beans cooked in coconut sauce – a hearty dish rich in carbohydrates and protein, perfect after a hard day in the garden.

Ugali and a sauce made from dried fish

Life in rural Tanzania isn't easy, but the lifestyle and diet are not without their benefits. Across the country, villages where processed foods are scarce and people are active display low levels of cardiovascular disease, digestive health issues, and cancer. The phenomenon of good health even extends to the tribes partial to more extreme dining habits. The Maasai, surviving traditionally on an almost entirely carnivorous, high fat diet, are included, as are the Hadza, whose consumption of fresh food consists of an incredible twenty percent honey. It brings a new definition to the term sweet tooth and illustrates that there is still a lot to learn about when it comes to our understanding of health, nutrition, and the human body.

Bright smiles of a healthy elderly couple still tending their farm daily

Contrary to common misconceptions, in many ways, the people here are living great lives. While the modern Western diet is linked to numerous health problems, the food in Tanzania is about as dissimilar as any could be. The lifestyle is active, communal, and over time, farmers have adopted staple crops suited to the climate, securing a relatively stable food supply. However, farming is basic, and the crops vulnerable to the elements, so when natural disasters occur, there are very few resources with which to respond. Still, a great deal is achieved with very little, nonetheless.

What works and what doesn't

If something should be changed in this system, it is not necessarily adopting modern practices or technologies. It is an interesting point to consider that

Cassava crop among native vegetation

international aid to developing countries is often delivered accompanied with the assumption that all cultures should follow in the developmental path carved out by the West – but should they?

Many cultures do not want to be modernised nor need to be. Examples of traditional farming systems that produce excellent yields can be found all over the world. However, some are more sustainable than others.

With sprawling terrain dominated by grasslands taller than themselves, farmers across Kigoma have long practiced slash and burn farming - a form of shifting agriculture where areas are cleared and burned to prepare land for cultivation. When using this technique, the ash of the burned vegetation adds a temporary increase of fertility to the soil, but this only lasts a season or two before it is depleted, and the farmers must move on to new areas.

The unsustainability of slash and burn farming lies in increasing population density. In centuries past, the practice worked reasonably well. With a sparse population, it was possible to leave the plots cleared for cropping undisturbed to recover for up

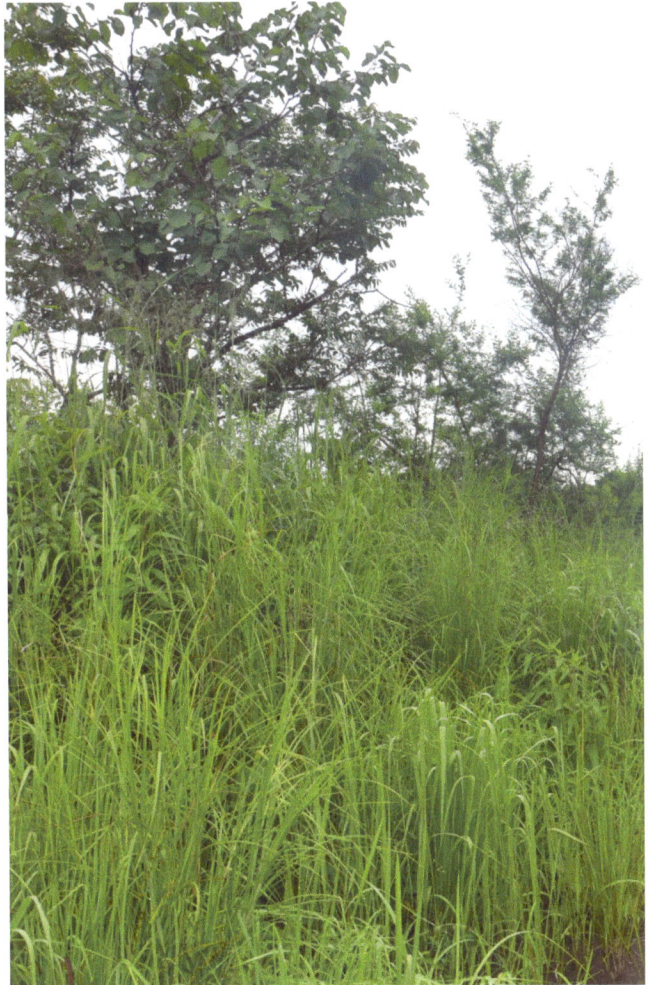

Many farming sites start dominated by grasslands

Site slashed ready to be burnt

Burning debris is the final step to prepare farm sites

Children playing among the flames while farm area is burnt

to twenty years. This fallow period allowed for considerable natural vegetation regrowth and restoration of the area's natural soil fertility.

Unfortunately, with an increasing population, the land is now needing to be reused much sooner. In addition, tropical rains quickly wash nutrients from soils, and larger trees do not have time to recolonise to produce leaf litter which reinvigorates the nutrient cycle. As a result, the practice is now contributing to a decline in both arable land and biodiversity.

Sustainability aside, slash and burn farming can be a dangerous business. For the villages around Kigoma, the practice is often a family affair. It is not unusual to see young children among the flames when areas are being cleared and burn injuries are common. Despite the dangers, all going well, a plot will be cleared and planted with a crop of the farmer's choosing. In the case of maharage, individuals will navigate their fields with a bag of beans and a hoe. Placing a handful of beans in their mouths, the farmers will sow the area, methodically chipping out planting holes with their hoes before spitting in a seed and drawing back a covering of soil.

It is a slow but effective process. The farmers have their hands free to till the planting holes, and each bean is deposited with a small amount of valuable moisture in the form of saliva. With luck, there will be some subsequent rain in the following days, and if so, a field of bean plants will germinate and emerge. Rain

Maharage crop fed by nutrients left in ash after burning

Man extracting beans from their dried pods

and good fortune play a part throughout the entire production cycle of maharage, from germination to processing. If the season is moist enough to sustain the plot without flooding and damaging the plants, a healthy crop of beans will be harvested. To do this, entire plants are uprooted and left to dry in the field. During this time, rain is the last thing any farmer wants. Moisture during the drying period carries the risk of the harvest becoming diseased or, worse still, germinating before being collected.

If the crop dries sufficiently, farmers and villagers enter the next phase of processing. First, the dry plants are collected and piled, then the hard work begins. The plants are repeatedly beaten with a large pole, expelling the prized beans from their dried pods. When the villagers are happy that most of the beans have been released, they remove the lighter vegetative material revealing the heavy beans below. The harvest is then cleaned and packed, ready for storage or transport to market.

There is no denying there are processes for food production in place and effective around the villages of Kigoma. Still, there is certainly room for improvement in their safety, sustainability, and variety. With the reliance on just a handful of staple crops, food security in this pocket of Tanzania is less of a concern than nutritional diversity. Therefore, the most valuable aid provided at a village level is not necessarily finance but education in alternative production techniques and seeds to diversify the fresh produce available in the resulting farming systems.

Men examining the quality of the processed beans

Ikabulu vegetable garden

Challenges moving forward

This is precisely what has occurred in the small and remote village of Ikabulu in the Kigoma region, where demonstration vegetable gardens have been set up to provide various produce and illustrate alternatives to slash and burn farming. Unlike slash and burn agriculture, at the Ikabulu gardens, old crops and pulled weeds are allowed to decompose in the gardens' compost bays. They are then reintroduced to the soil as nutrient-rich organic matter, enabling the site to be cultivated and productive indefinitely.

Man tending to sustainably grown crops

OFF THE GARDEN PATH

Crop rotation is the process of altering the type of vegetables growing in each bed, each season, and is invaluable in sustainable subsistence farming. Different vegetables exploit or return nutrients to the soil as the rotations occur, and the practice also aids in stopping insect pests from getting too comfortable in any one area. The Ikabulu gardens were set up to demonstrate this process and other sustainable practices, including mulching and raised beds.

While introducing new varieties of vegetables might seem straightforward, this aspect of the gardens has posed unexpected challenges. One reason the crops already grown across Kigoma have been adopted and maintained is that they are relatively pest and disease resistant. So, new and exotic vegetables are often as enticing for the region's insects as they are for the people.

The biodiversity in the Kigoma region is astonishing. Beautiful butterflies and moths the size of small plates add to its wild ambience, but for gardeners, this means caterpillars - and big ones. Caterpillars aren't the region's only large residents. Measuring up to an enormous twenty centimetres, the giant African land snail (*Achatina fulica*) also lurks in the thick vegetation. At night the jungle and savannah come alive with the calls of thousands of insects. It is, again, a wonderful experience for visitors, but in the gardens, sunrise reveals what new vegetables are likely to be a long-term success and the unfortunate remains of those more likely to feed pests than people.

Ikabulu's biodiversity is wonderful

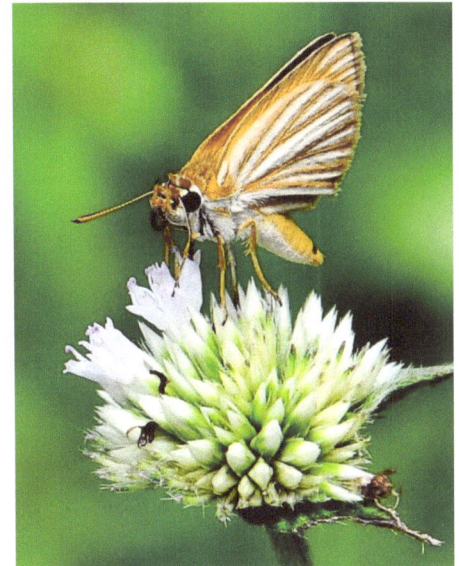

Butterfly on flower of *Ethulia* sp.

Children learning new gardening techniques

One of Ikabulu's vegetable gardens has been installed at the local school to demonstrate alternative production practices to the next generation who can carry them on. In remote villages like Ikabulu, it is a feat to have a school at all. If one exists, it is just as challenging to encourage children to attend, so the inclusion of a practical vegetable garden serves many purposes. Not only is the site productive and an example of sustainable gardening, but it presents a break from the classroom, offering students a chance to learn something directly relevant to their lives at home.

From the sky, the African tropical savannah is a wonder so green it would be easy to mistake it for a wilderness yet to be discovered by humans. However, the true wonder is experienced below. Not only do people live here, but they have largely tamed their inhospitable surroundings. Everyone you meet is a gardener and has been their entire lives, so it is probably no coincidence that the people of Ikabulu also offer up some of the brightest smiles you'll ever see.

It is proof positive that there really is something to be said for living a simple life. But deep down, isn't that something gardeners know already?

Students presenting some of the garden's harvest

OFF THE GARDEN PATH

Gardens Born of Practicality
The Living Bridges of Sohra
Meghalaya, India

A nation of gardening extremes, from indulgent to obscure

As one of the world's largest and most populous countries, horticultural diversity is a natural accompaniment to the colour and vibrancy of India. From weedy verges in the dusty and crowded streets of its cities to rural areas where people embrace agriculture with both hands, plants are ever present, but amenity horticulture can seem sparse. Looking deeper, however, and when ornamental gardening is executed in India, the results are incredibly well presented and often display grandeur to rival the world's best.

Heavily influenced by empires of the past, including the Moghuls and the British, India possesses stunning historical architecture and gardens that have been established to match. These gardens are designed to impress, whether through immaculately kept hedges and topiary or extravagant annual exhibitions of seasonal colour. Established throughout centuries past, many of India's grand gardens were created for the sole purpose of conveying a sense of wealth and opulence to visitors and are so detailed, they would not survive today if not for the country's overflowing labour force.

Incidentally, the historical pattern to accompany grand architecture with gardens to match appears somewhat understated at one of India's most iconic and revered landmarks. Located at Agra in the state of Uttar Pradesh - the Taj Mahal is synonymous with India and attracts millions of visitors annually. The marble mausoleum famed around the world has a history of romance and tragedy, befitting the splendour of the structure. Still, the surrounding grounds are strangely restrained, by comparison, presented in a somewhat simple style of Indo-Persian influence. The entire site is an example of exquisite design, and it could be argued that the grounds have been maintained with minimalist landscaping to enhance the

Victoria Memorial, Kolkata is one of India's great gardens

impact of the Taj Mahal itself. However, there could be more to this story and another explanation – an explanation that challenges the very history of the site and a widely accepted myth surrounding its conception.

Unearthing a ghost of gardening past

The Taj Mahal was commissioned early in the seventeenth century CE by the Mughal Emperor Shah Jahan to house the remains of the emperor's favourite of three wives, Mumtaz Mahal, after she died prematurely during the birth of the pair's fourteenth child. This was a romantic gesture in itself, but as the story goes, Shah Jahan intended to cement the couple's relationship in history by constructing a second identical mausoleum to be built entirely out of black marble. Housing his remains, this structure would mirror the Taj Mahal from across the nearby Yamuna River, allowing the couple to look upon one another for eternity. Unfortunately, Jahan was usurped and imprisoned by his son before any construction could occur and spent his last years under house arrest.

An endearing tale still passed on as truth, this legend adds to the romance surrounding the Taj Mahal but appears to have been born of fiction as much as fact. His son certainly imprisoned Emperor Shah Jahan, but somewhat disappointingly, it is increasingly doubtful that there was ever an intention to build a second Taj Mahal. Archaeological research at the site of the supposed black mausoleum has instead uncovered the remains of something extraordinary in its own right - the Mehtab Bagh or 'Moonlight Garden'.

Now thought to have been designed as the ultimate viewing point to gaze out to the Taj Mahal, the Mehtab Bagh was virtually washed away during various floods and buried deep under alluvial soils during the last century. As a result, archaeologists had to remove over ninety thousand cubic metres of earth from the area before being able to piece together the remnants of the once extensive gardens.

With the black Taj Mahal theory largely discredited and the cultural significance of the Mehtab Bagh enthusiastically accepted, efforts have been made to restore the gardens to their former glory. Reclaiming its title as a fantastic vantage point to view the Taj Mahal once more, the Mehtab Bagh has been replanted

View of the Taj Mahal from the Mehtab Bagh

Structure and flood wall at the Mehtab Bagh

with favourites of the Moghul era. From daffodils (*Narcissus* spp.), oleanders (*Nerium oleander*), and guavas (*Psidium guajava*) to orchid trees (*Bauhinia variegata*), ashoka (*Saraca asoca*), and a multitude of *Hibiscus* species, the Mehtab Bagh is awash with blooms that glow at twilight. It is again living up to its long-forgotten name.

There are charming gardens to rival the Mehtab Bagh to be found across India, which command attention and awaken the senses. It is undeniable that civilisation has had a long and successful relationship with amenity horticulture in this part of the world but tucked far away in the northeastern highlands of the country, there stand gardens like no others. Gardens that were born of necessity and practicality, without a thought for any ornamental appeal but gardens that now, ironically, draw thousands of visitors each year just for the views.

A little-known paradise

As the cultural corridor between India and Southeast Asia, the expanse of land known as Northeast India offers an atmospheric encounter unlike any of its neighbours. Geopolitically complex and home to over one hundred different ethnic groups, the mountainous antecedent to the Himalayas is a repository of the extraordinary. Comprised of eight official states, the regions of Northeast India are diverse, from their cultures and cuisine to their flora and fauna.

Though the pocket of earth bordered by Bhutan, Bangladesh, Myanmar, and China has experienced relatively little international exposure, the states that form Northeast India account for nearly ten percent of the country's landmass. Together these states possess a haven of biodiversity and accommodate around fifty percent of the nation's plant species, including close to one thousand orchid

View over Meghalaya at sunset

Khasi women selling orchids at market in Shillong

species. This impressive figure is complemented with over one thousand butterfly species, just as many birds and hundreds of endemic herptiles.

Once comprised of only seven states (Arunachal Pradesh, Assam, Manipur, Meghalaya, Mizoram, Nagaland, and Tripura), Northeast India was known as the land of the seven sisters. However, it expanded with an eighth state in nineteen seventy-five when the previously sovereign Kingdom of Sikkim became recognised as a formalised portion of India. The eight states of the region are remarkably well forested and are continually vying for the title of the 'greenest place in India' – a claim not so easily determined.

Dominating in the sheer volume of its forests, Arunachal Pradesh consists of around seventy square kilometres of greenspace, but it is also the largest of the Northeast Indian states. Mizoram is much smaller by comparison, but close to ninety percent of the state is under forest cover. So, which is greener? It is semantic quibbling really and the dominance of lush vegetation is a distinct feature throughout the entire region. Furthermore, Meghalaya, one of the most beautiful of the states, has never held any particular title regarding its floral bounty. Still, it is sought out as the benchmark wild and green destination over all others. So perhaps the title 'greenest place in India' carries little advantage.

Meghalaya can be roughly translated to mean 'abode in the clouds' and receiving well over ten metres of rainfall annually, the hills and valleys in this state are considered some of the wettest places on the planet. The abundant water supply is reflected in the vigour of the vegetation that blankets the terrain. It is here that intrepid gardeners, adventurers, and trekkers alike, come to witness the wildly unique gardens known as the 'living bridges of Sohra'.

Areca palm plantation in the hills of Meghalaya

From the relaxed tone in the capital of Shillong to its serene mountain villages, Meghalaya has an atmosphere of its own and is a world away from conventional India. The population heralds from various tribes, but the Khasi ethnic group is most dominant and accounts for around fifty percent of the state's population. Khasi culture and cuisine add immensely to the ambience of Meghalaya. There is an air of ease in the cities, and nothing seems too urgent, while in rural villages, the attitude is much the same, and life is traditionally simple.

The hill tribes of Meghalaya, including the Khasis, not only contribute to the flavours and way of life in this part of the world, but over centuries they have also altered the landscape with surreal results. Life in one of the wettest places on Earth comes with its share of challenges, and one of the most significant has been how to traverse the region's abundance of monsoonal rivers and streams. Bridges would seem the obvious answer, but when conditions are as wet, and flash floods as frequent as they are in Meghalaya, the longevity of any construction is short. High in the hills of Northeast India, an ingenious solution to overcome these issues has been embraced. Here, bridges aren't built; they're grown.

A unique part of the world with crops to match

There are living bridges scattered throughout Meghalaya, but those in the surrounds of the high-altitude town of Sohra, are the grandest. The extraordinary feats of both man and nature are part of everyday transit for remote villagers, but for visitors, access to many of the sites can be challenging and often includes navigating steep slopes amidst thick vegetation. Many living bridges involve several hours of arduous trekking and are isolated far from any vehicle access. However, in the mountains of Meghalaya, the journey offers as much as the destination.

Dispersed throughout the jungle, small villages remain inconspicuous and virtually undetectable, aside from moss-covered stone tracks, until the undergrowth opens out and a greater human influence in the landscape is revealed. One of the first hints that a village may be nearby in the Meghalayan jungle is the sudden prevalence of areca palms (*Areca catechu*). The plants are prolific, and it would be easy to assume they are naturally occurring, but the palms are actually arranged into orchards of sorts, carefully tended to, allocated, and owned. Some townships are closer to areca plantations which house a few custodians, than they are villages and the communities rely solely on the income gained through the sale of the species. The timber of the areca palm is a useful material in construction, and the plant's fronds can be fashioned into environmentally friendly serving dishes,

Pineapple (*Ananas comosus*)

Jackfruit (*Artocarpus heterophyllus*)

Areca palm fruit

Aging scaffolding on the journey to the living bridges

but these are only by-products. The primary reason for areca cultivation is the narcotic kernel within its fruit.

Hugely popular across Southeast Asia and Oceania, *A. catechu* is traditionally combined with slaked lime and the leaf of the betel vine (*Piper betel*), then chewed. The combination of compounds reacts to cause a profusion of red saliva and provides the user with a mild and warming psychoactive effect lasting several minutes. Highly addictive, in many countries, areca nut chewing is as common as a cup of coffee, though the practice presents side effects from stained teeth and tooth decay to cancer.

View from below the living bridges

The legendary double decker living bridges

Areca palm plantations are a sign of changing times in the hills of Meghalaya. Populations have grown steadily over recent decades, putting pressure on villages and traditional lifestyles. Many communities have opted to move from subsistence gardens which had sustained rural populations for centuries, to monocultural plantations of cash crops. *A. catechu* is not the only high-value and low input crop that thrives in the northeast of India. Cashews (*Anacardium occidentale*), rubber (*Hevea brasiliensis*),

Broom grass (*Thysanolaena maxima*) drying for sale

The hills of Meghalaya are littered with cave networks

Ancient fossils in Arwah Cave, Sohra

tea (*Camellia sinensis*), coffee (*Coffea* spp.), and broom grass (*Thysanolaena maxima*), as well as a variety of fruits, are grown for commercial purposes, finding their way into local, national and international markets.

Exotic crops aside, the journeys to many living bridges are made all the more venturesome because of the prehistoric-looking landscape. Some living bridges require traversing sheer cliff faces by climbing across decaying timber scaffolding, and fossil-filled cave networks add to the atmosphere. The Umshiang double-decker root bridge, perhaps the most impressive of the living bridges, requires visitors to navigate over two and a half thousand steps, including several forming near-vertical climbs, through a landscape as ancient as it is beautiful.

Ingenuity and innovation utilising a biological marvel

Aside from the occasional dizzying view and heart-pounding climb, journeying among the jungle presents a serene experience. Accompanied by the chirping of the area's numerous endemic bird species, the sound of running water is never far away. Owing to Sohra's relentless rainfall, rivers, streams, and waterfalls are typical of the region's character and go hand in hand with the living bridges. The scenes work in harmony

Crystal clear waters of the Umngot River

Waterfalls go hand in hand with the living bridges

and are the ultimate in biophilic green architecture. In fact, when arriving at a bridge for the first time, it takes some evaluation and adjustment in thinking to realise the scenery has been subjected to any form of human alteration at all.

Indian rubber trees (*Ficus elastica*) are common among the thick vegetation of Meghalaya. Known as facultative hemi-epiphytes, the plants possess ingenious adaptations for survival. Spread by birds, the plant's seeds are dispersed onto branches of other trees high up in the forest canopy where they germinate, and *F. elastica* begins its early stages of life as an epiphyte. Nestled on the limbs of a supportive host, *F. elastica* is not a parasite and does not draw its nutrient from other plants. Instead, it produces an

The Ummunoi living bridge is one of India's oldest

Bridges are first formed with roots only millimetres thick

Flexible roots soon turn to rigid supports

An example of inosculation

extensive network of fast-growing roots that extract water and nutrients from the air and any nearby surfaces.

This unorthodox start to life allows *F. elastica* to utilise the light in the canopy it would not receive on the forest floor while producing roots growing toward the soil aided by gravity. Once these roots hit the ground, the plant remains in ample light but achieves a significant increase in water and nutrients. The plants can then become so vigorous they quickly engulf the original tree on which they germinated.

It was this speed of growth and the malleability of aerial roots that early, innovative tribes in Meghalaya noticed as a potential resource. Where cut timber would rot and decay in the monsoonal rains, living material would only grow and become stronger in the conditions, so the concept of constructing living bridges using the roots of *F. elastica* was born.

Besides the plant's rapid growth and tendency to bed down its extensive network of aerial roots wherever they are directed, *F. elastica* possesses another characteristic that allows for the construction of living bridges - it can inosculate. Inosculation is the process by which plant tissues fuse either on a single specimen or between several plants. This means that multiple stems and roots can unite when held in contact, forming singular strengthened structures. It is difficult to believe that the immense bridges of fused tissues, some of which can support over fifty people at once, were initially trained using roots no more than a few millimetres thick.

While the living bridges of Sohra and its surroundings are a world away from conventional gardens, many aspects that need to be considered by the bridge gardeners are the same considerations needed for anyone tending a garden. The bridges need to be planned, trained, and pruned, even if the trees are already growing in the desired location, and if not, the initial plants need to be nursed, planted, and the site's fertility considered to ensure the efficient growth of the bridge. The construction of living bridges is not a quick process. The foresight required at the conceptual stage is astonishing and speaks volumes about the resourceful ingenuity of past and present Khasi generations.

When initially constructing a bridge, various techniques can be used to direct the roots of *F. elastica*. Sometimes, the roots of the trees are simply pulled, tied, and twisted by hand to encourage them to fuse. Other root bridges have been made using areca palm and bamboo scaffolds. The young roots are guided out across these temporary structures, with the perishable scaffolds replaced many times during the formation of the completed bridge as they rot in the heavy monsoon rains. Using existing trees, living root bridges can take fifteen years or more before the bridges are strong enough to support humans. They then become more robust every year, and some of the bridges around Sohra are thought to be well over five hundred years old.

Umkar root bridge displaying the techniques involved in the formation of root bridges

As society changes across Meghalaya, the construction of new bridges is rare, but one outstanding example of a recent project can be found at the village of Umkar. This bridge is not entirely new and more of a repair. A previous living bridge was badly damaged in flash flooding at the site, but it provides a great example of how roots are trained and guided, displaying various stages of inosculation. The people of Umkar have also chosen to upgrade the original bridge with recent training appearing to form a complex multi-directional bridge system. The bridge will take at least another decade before it is functional, but the gardeners' patience pays off in the long run when it comes to growing living bridges.

Within an hour's walk of the newly establishing Umkar bridge stands one of the region's oldest - Ummunoi. Ummunoi is an excellent demonstration of what a few hundred years of growth will achieve at Umkar. Ummunoi looks truly primordial. Its once minuscule roots are now firmly fused into well-formed walls, more than a metre thick in places and covered in a healthy coat of moss. Ummunoi's bare structure remains natural and exposed while other older bridges support clay coatings on their bases which allow

The Ummunoi living bridge has only gained strength with age

a smoother walk for villagers and add to an overall synthesis with the surrounding landscape. However, this custom has come at a cost to bridges in the past when mud and rocks have needed to be removed after causing structural damage, so the practice is now uncommon.

Ancient relics with an uncertain future

The root bridges of Meghalaya come in a variety of shapes and sizes. They are unique examples of botanical architecture that have been grown without the tools of modern engineering. Some have been known to extend to over fifty metres, while others hang more than twenty metres above the streams they

Mud coatings on bridges are uncommon due to the weight involved

cross. Many support everyday traffic across a single span, though others are more complex and consist of multiple levels. Regardless of appearance, Meghalaya's living bridges are an important glimpse into the past and a possible resource for the future.

The practice of creating new living bridges and of preserving those already in existence had dwindled during the twentieth century, slowly fading out with societal change. In fact, in many villages across the region, root bridges are little more than a memory. However, early in the twenty-first century, the bridges began drawing national and international attention as outstanding tourist attractions. The renewed interest spurred local dedication to the structures, keeping some from being destroyed in favour of steel alternatives and even inspiring the construction of a handful of new ones.

In addition to drawing in tourists, the root bridges have also attracted the interest of scientists in recent years, with expeditions yielding valuable results. Not only have researchers examined and recorded the location of over seventy living bridges in Meghalaya, but by speaking with village elders, they have also been able to document the traditional bridge-building techniques of the Khasi. Very little about the construction processes has ever been recorded in writing, with the practices traditionally demonstrated and verbally explained between villagers. So, this was a significant achievement in ensuring the bridges can continue to be established in the future.

There are numerous examples of living architecture worldwide. However, living root bridges provide the only known example of the repeated, predictable use of tree growth for structural purposes. The processes may have architectural applications far beyond the hills of Meghalaya. Whatever lies ahead for the living bridge concept, the bridges in existence will live for as long as the organisms that they have been formed from remain healthy. Some are thought to be over five hundred years old, while others have only just been constructed, and many more fit somewhere in between. So, it is fair to say no matter what the future holds, the living bridges of Meghalaya will likely continue to inspire wonder in the eyes of the world throughout our lifetimes and beyond.

The Ummunoi bridge has stood for several hundred years

Gardens Without Gardeners
Himalayan Rhododendron Forests
Gandaki Zone, Nepal

Horticulture at altitude

Rich in natural beauty, there are many reasons to visit the Southeast Asian nation of Nepal. Setting foot in the country, perched high in the Himalayas, it is quickly apparent that spirituality is central to Nepali society and a key ingredient in its character. A land of pagodas and monasteries, Nepal is an important location for both the Hindu and Buddhist religions. Adorning the mountains, brightly coloured Buddhist prayer flags can be seen strung across vast expanses accompanied by shrines and prayer wheels. At the same time, statues of Hindu deities greased with offerings are commonplace in the cities, complementing an array of ancient temples. These holy sites attract thousands of devotees from around the world each year. The country also plays host to the mighty Mount Everest. Standing over eight thousand metres above sea level, the mountain is Earth's tallest and, for thrill-seeking adventurers, offers a different pilgrimage altogether.

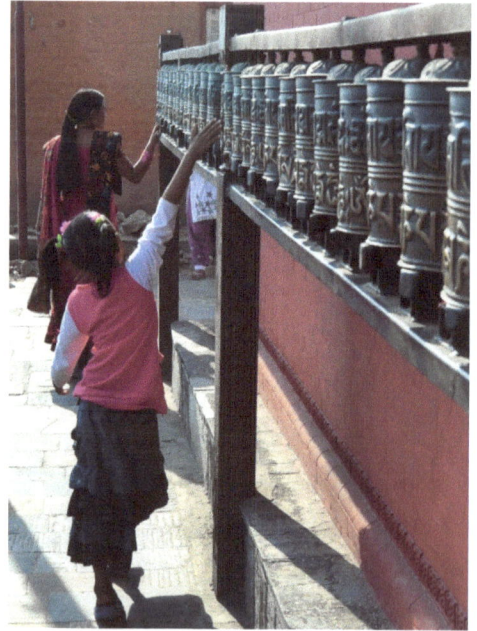

Girl spins Buddhist prayer wheels in Kathmandu

Nepali architecture at Pashupatinath Temple, a sacred site for the Hindu religion

Influenced by dramatic changes in altitude, Nepal's geography and environmental conditions are as diverse as the scenery that they foster. The nation's capital Kathmandu offers a mild and temperate climate, perfect for gardens but has grown to become an expanse of paved and sealed surfaces like many large cities. As a result, one of the most popular ways to foster plants in this region is using pots and containers. Upon first impression, the populous city can seem a little barren, but there is an undeniable gardening culture among Kathmandu's residents. Whether on rooftops, balconies, or ledges, plants can be seen carefully tended to and nurtured. There are also more extensive formal gardens and parks to be found across the city and its fringes. Of these, the most popular is the aptly named Garden of Dreams. At over one hundred years old, this neo-classical garden displays an Edwardian influence and provides a dreamlike oasis tucked away from the noise and chaos of the surrounding streets.

Hindu deities are commonly seen adorned with offerings

Potted garden in Bhaktapur

The Garden of Dreams

Consisting of six pavilions, the site has also been known as the Garden of Six Seasons. Each pavilion represents one of the six climatic periods recognised in Nepal, basanta (spring), grishma (early summer), barkha (summer monsoon), sharad (early autumn), hemanta (late autumn), and shishir (winter). Within the garden's walls, decorative furniture is accompanied by pergolas, water features, and birdhouses. Creeping figs (*Ficus pumila*) have been used extensively, providing a blanket of green on most vertical surfaces, and everything is immaculately maintained. Shrub topiaries mimicking clouds and rose-covered arbours add to the romance of the scene. So, it is no wonder the Garden of Dreams is a popular spot for young Nepali couples to meet.

Cloud pruned shrubs are meticulously maintained to complement the landscape

Views are spectacular higher in the Himalayas of Nepal and the Annapurna Circuit

Farming practices honed over centuries

However, while pleasant, it is not the gardens of Kathmandu that draw the attention of plant lovers to Nepal. High up in the mountains, gardens of beauty to match the world's best have not been planted; they occur naturally. The rhododendron forests of Nepal swathe the mountainous slopes with colour when spring arrives in the Himalayas. Extending for kilometre upon kilometre, the forests can be accessed by following several of Nepal's famous trekking routes. The Everest Base Camp trail is an arduous trekking mecca for dedicated adventurers, but more accessible hikes, which include the rhododendron forests and require less effort, can be found around the picturesque city of Pokhara in the heart of the country.

Farmers regulate water flow with swales and terraces

Chitwan National Park

Average temperatures in Nepal drop by around six degrees (Celsius) for every thousand metre rise in altitude. When ascending to the Annapurna Massif in central Nepal, the environment changes considerably. Kathmandu and Pokhara are situated at similar elevations of around one thousand and four hundred metres above sea level, but one of the most popular routes between the destinations involves descending through the Chitwan region near the Indian border. At just over four hundred metres above sea level, Chitwan National Park has a tropical monsoonal climate and is humid throughout the year. As a result, the plants occurring there are quite different from those found in the rhododendron forests.

From Kathmandu to Chitwan and climbing toward Pokhara, the climate is ideal for a range of valuable food crops. The tropical environment around Chitwan is perfectly suited to rice (*Oryza sativa*) farming, but with rising altitude and dropping average temperatures, the crops grown in the terraced gardens etched into the mountainsides become more varied. By nature, human existence in the Himalayas is challenging. The topographical extremes have meant people have had to become innovative in all facets of life, including food production. Nepal's terraced gardens are a perfect example of necessity proving to be the mother of invention.

Ancient terraced gardens have been found worldwide, from Asia, Africa, and South America to the Mediterranean Basin. However, it is unlikely any individuals passed on the building techniques across the continents. Instead, terraced gardens appear to offer an example of different cultures using the same option to solve comparable environmental problems at similar points in time. In this instance, the creation of level gardens reinforced with stone and clay on sloped surfaces was adopted to increase arable land.

Palaeoethnobotanical research has indicated that agriculture has been commonplace in the Himalayas for at least three thousand years. Prehistoric seed and plant material found in the area tell a story of how the civilisations of the mountains went from utilising a handful of staple crops to embracing an increasing diversity of species as centuries passed. For generations, people of the Himalayas have developed indigenous knowledge of terrace management. From matching the ideal height and width of retaining walls to the particular gradient of the land to slowing excess water movement using vegetated clay bunding, terrace farming may appear simple, but complex biophysical practices are involved. Though the tradition dates back centuries, terrace farming remains a viably sustainable form of agriculture today, restraining, even reversing, land degradation and erosion.

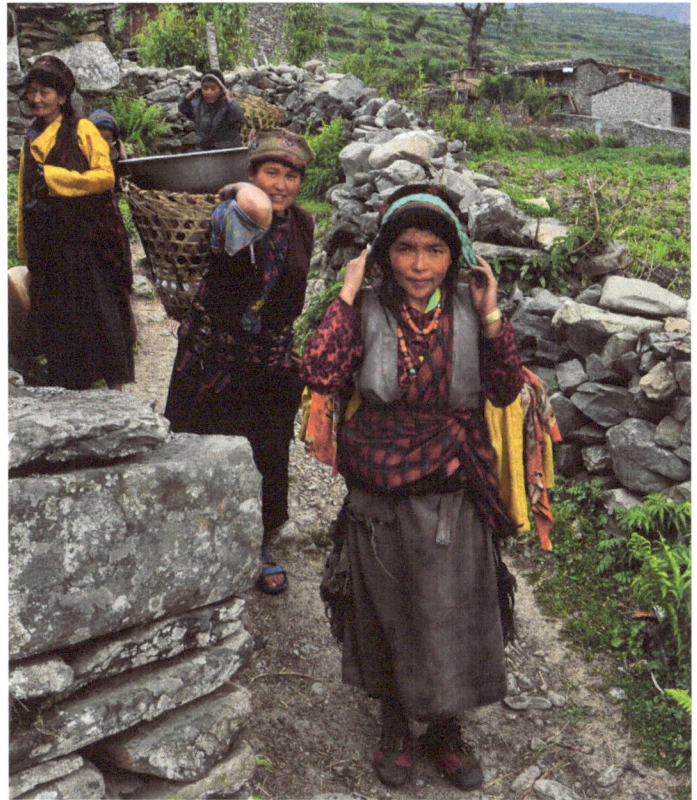

Woman transporting goods on foot

Terraced farms are standard scenery on the ascent into the peaks of the Himalayas

Changing colours with the seasons

Flowers of the tree rhododendron
(*Rhododendron arboreum*)

Extensively utilised, terraced farms are all to be seen in some areas of central Nepal until, at altitudes of around one thousand and four hundred metres, rhododendron forests enter the landscape. Often intertwined with the man-made terrace farms, these forests extend to the extremes of the plants' range at just over three and a half thousand metres above sea level. The name rhododendron is derived from the Greek words rhodos (meaning rose) and dendron (meaning tree), referring to the large and profuse blooms of the genus. There are over one thousand naturally occurring species of rhododendron and exceedingly popular with gardeners around the world, tens of thousands of cultivated varieties. Of these, thirty species can be found in Nepal, but it is a single species for which the region is most famous. So ingrained in the country's culture that it is Nepal's national flower, the tree rhododendron (*Rhododendron arboreum*) is the dominant species of the forests and provides the majority of the mountains' spring colour.

In gardens around the world, *R. arboreum* is considered an indicator of taste and class, but in Nepal, the plant's value lies in far more than just its ornamental appeal. The wood is used for construction, furniture, and creating smaller utensils. The flowers are prepared into teas, preserves, or eaten fresh and have also been used to treat dysentery. Even the leaves of the plant have some value as stock fodder.

Colour on mass, it is hard to believe the rhododendrons of Nepal weren't planted

OFF THE GARDEN PATH

When it comes to the edibility of its flowers, *R. arboreum* is an exception within the *Rhododendron* genus, and great care is taken to ensure the blooms are taken from the correct species before they are consumed. In general, all parts of most *Rhododendron* species are toxic, with poisoning in both humans and livestock regularly occurring. Even the nectar and pollen collected by bees foraging among some rhododendrons can transfer this toxicity to the resulting honey created in the bees' hives. In Nepal, this is known as 'mad honey' and, in some cases, is deliberately produced as it has a psychoactive effect and is used in traditional medicine.

The molecule responsible for poisoning is a neurotoxin known as grayanotoxin, which affects the central nervous system. It is strong enough to kill honeybees though many have developed some form of resistance. In commercial honey production, any contaminated honey would be mixed with large volumes of variously sourced clean honey, nullifying any toxicity. However, in Nepal, producers foster small hives foraging only among the toxic rhododendrons, resulting in a potent concentration of grayanotoxin.

The physiology of *R. arboreum* is as variable as its uses. The plants growing at lower temperate altitudes produce the iconic vibrant red flowers admired around the world. Remarkably, as altitude increases, the flowers of the same species intriguingly begin shifting to shades of pink before gradually becoming entirely white when growing at the sub-alpine elevations approaching the species' upper limits.

The toxicity of *R. arboreum* foliage as livestock fodder is also variable but not due to altitude. While the flowers of the species are not considered toxic and are readily consumed by people in Nepal, the suitability of the plant's leaves as animal feed depends on the seasons. In the winter months, the fresh leaves exhibit little toxicity and suffice as a supplementary food option when other sources of sustenance are scarce. However, as the plants enter

Rhododendron arboreum can display blooms from white and pink to red

The moss-covered tree rhododendrons create a trekking atmosphere like nothing else

their reproductive cycle and produce spring flowers, the foliage of *R. arboreum* becomes increasingly toxic, deterring any grazing animals from eating the plant and its valuable blooms.

In addition, *R. arboreum* is physiologically variable in form and height, depending on the plants' location. Sheltered adult plants occurring in good soils can appear as large gnarled trees, reaching up to twenty-five metres in height, while specimens growing in poorer soils and exposed to the elements may take the form of smaller shrubs.

The plants are notoriously slow-growing, taking upwards of twenty years before they first flower, and it can be up to fifty years before the trees develop into their final mature form. With changing land use and the utilisation of *R. arboreum* as a source of timber, it is hard to gauge the age to which the species can grow, but specimens well over one hundred years old have been documented. Covered in moss and displaying layers of flaking bark, the contorted branches of the trees impart a magically ancient ambience in the rhododendron forests. Indeed, the forests are ancient, and fossils from the area from around fifty million years ago resemble species existing in nature today. The fascinating finds have been invaluable in piecing together the history of the rhododendron and suggest that it was in the Himalayas that the flamboyant plants originally evolved.

With their dominating and tortured forms each tree is unique

Flowers of Himalayan primrose *(Primula denticulata)*

Pieris formosa, native to Nepal

Forests of unrivalled beauty

Another *Rhododendron* species likely to be encountered while traversing the rhododendron forests is the scarlet flowered *R. barbatum*, which increases in prevalence at altitudes above two and a half thousand metres and is often seen mixed with silver fir *(Abies spectabilis)*. At even higher altitudes, *R. campanulatum* is common, but it is not just the rhododendrons that make the Himalayas a floral paradise. Nepal is teeming with native plant species that are highly ornamental. Due to its remarkable changes in altitude and geography, the country possesses six vegetation zones: tropical, sub-tropical, low temperate, high temperate, subalpine, and alpine flora. As a result, the country is innately biodiverse.

Accompanying rhododendrons, other members of the Ericaceae family frequent the Himalayan landscape, including species of *Pieris* and *Gaultheria*. The graceful shrub *Viburnum erubescens*, with its showers of delicate flowers, is widespread in the region, and looking to the forest floor, there are all manner of herbaceous plant species. However, there are times when the Himalayas are clearly at their

Iris kemaonensis is a high-altitude iris

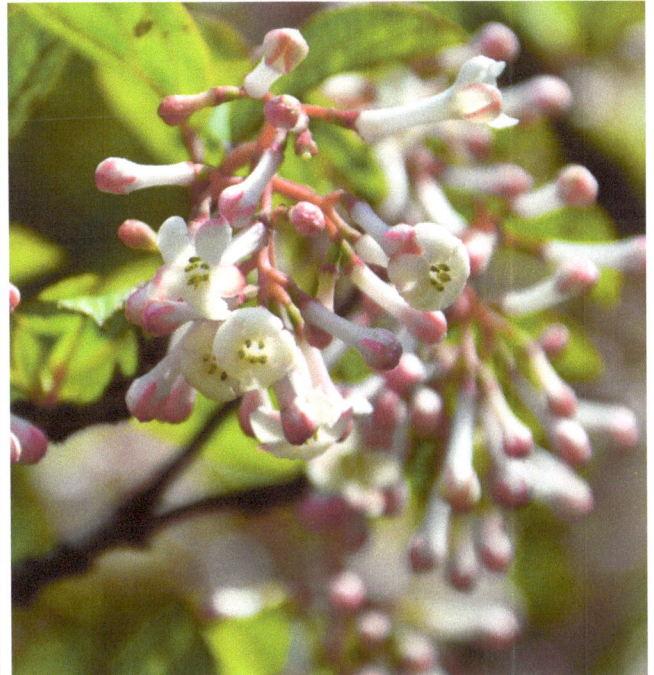
Delicate blooms of *Viburnum erubescens*

botanical best in the quest for plants. *Viburnum erubescens* and many plants found in Nepal are deciduous and dormant over winter. Herbaceous perennials are plants that die back to an underground storage organ when dormant and include one of the Himalayan highlights, *Iris kemaonensis*, a high-altitude iris seen from Tibetan China, Bhutan, and India to Nepal. It would be difficult to know it existed for much of the year, so spring is undoubtedly the season for budding botanists to visit the mountains.

Displaying spectacular views of the commanding peaks of Annapurna and Mount Everest, trekking the rhododendron forests of Nepal offers scenery of unmatched beauty that is the envy of gardeners around the world. Even the rhododendron collections in the gardens of the wealthiest aristocrat can't match the size and splendour of the naturally occurring populations in this part of the world.

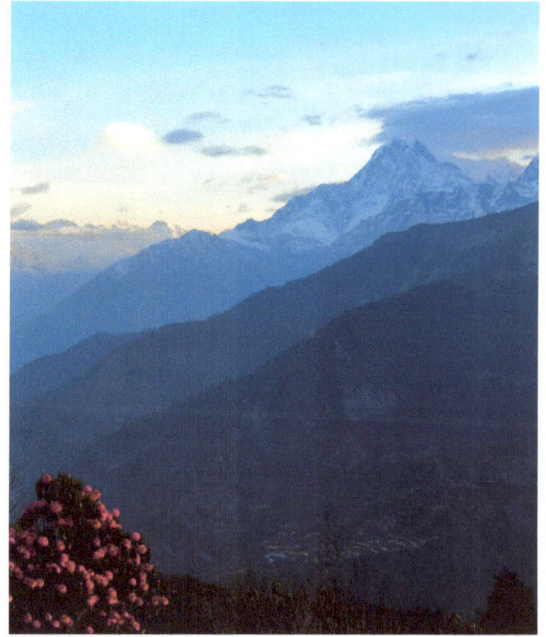

Rhododendrons occupy large stands along the Annapurna Circuit of Nepal

For centuries humans have endeavoured to master the natural environment and create magnificent gardens, each concept vying to be more spectacular than the next. While all along, Mother Nature herself had set the standard in grand gardens and with an extensive design romantically framed by snow-capped mountains of the Himalayas, were we ever really in contention?

View of Annapurna at sunrise

Changing a Culture
Mere's Gardens
Honiara, Solomon Islands

Nine distinct provinces

Isolated deep within the endless blue waters of the South Pacific Ocean lies an expanse of rugged and wild islands that appear almost forgotten in time. Consisting of nearly one thousand volcanic islands and coral atolls, the archipelagic nation of the Solomon Islands is home to beautiful coral reefs, picturesque waterfalls, and pristine montane cloud forest. Still, its existence is unknown to much of the world.

Crystal clear waters of the Solomon Islands

The country is divided into nine remote provinces, each with distinct landscapes, languages, and cultures. Situated roughly in the middle of the country and easiest to access by boat from the nation's only international airport are the tropical islands that make up the Central Province. This region is an excellent introduction to what can be expected across the Islands, offering colourful corals and unusual fauna, from hawksbill turtles (*Eretmochelys imbricata*) to Melanesian megapodes (*Megapodius eremita*).

Clown fish of the family Pomacentridae

Corals of the Central Province

Makira produces an extensive variety of bananas

Paper mulberry (*Broussonetia papyrifera*)

Melanesian megapodes are chicken-like birds that nest on sandy beaches, and in the Solomon Islands, their eggs are considered a valuable food source. The strangely elongated eggs can be found at markets across the country, but it is another product that dominates market stalls in the Makira Province.

With over eighty varieties of bananas recorded growing within its islands' shores, Makira provides a new appreciation for the humble fruit. Unlike the widely cultivated Cavendish (*Musa acuminata* 'Dwarf Cavendish'), the colours of Makira's bananas range from purples, reds, and yellows to greens and everything in between. They come in all shapes and sizes, and it has been suggested that uncatalogued varieties may yet number in the hundreds.

Though the Solomon Islands are considered part of Melanesia, the inhabitants of the Renbel Province in the south of the country are unique, as they are actually Polynesian. Across Polynesia, customary tattoos play an essential role in cultural traditions. The practice is also upheld in Renbel, where the unique markings are one of the population's most distinctive features. While heavy black neck and shoulder markings are still common, before the adoption of Christianity, the 'taukuka' tattooing practice was a painful rite of passage. Reserved only for those seen to have risen to chiefly status, this system of tattoos blackened the entirety of its recipients' neck, chest, arms, and torso.

The Polynesian influence on Renbel can also be seen in the customary use of 'tapa'. Made from the bark of the paper mulberry (*Broussonetia papyrifera*), tapa is a type of cloth used broadly across the region. The tree's bark is pounded and flattened through a long and laborious process until a soft, thin material is produced. In addition to traditional uses, tapa is used as the canvas material for artwork created and sold in the Solomon Islands. While as a province, Renbel and its population make up only a small portion of the nation, they contribute enormously to its character.

Tapa and tattoos unique to the Renbel Province

Bioluminescent fungi (*Mycena chlorophos*)

Cave systems are common in the Solomon Islands

The Wild West

Historically, countries the world over have encompassed brutal customs, and the Solomon Islands are no different. Headhunting was a common practice carried out throughout the islands and particularly in the trade waters surrounding the Isabel, Choiseul, and Western provinces. Invading groups navigating the islands in large sea-faring canoes would collect the heads of their victims. As a result, Isabel is well known for its skull shrines, but far from the past practices, its people are among the nation's most relaxed, friendly, and peace-loving.

To the far north of the Solomon Islands, nearing Bougainville and Papua New Guinea, stand the islands less travelled that make up the Choiseul Province. While the scenery is marvellous and flora diverse, Choiseul is also known for a past, not for the faint-hearted. Across Melanesia, headhunting was widespread and often accompanied by ritualistic cannibalism.

Skull shrine of the Western Province

Just how often cannibalism occurred remains contentious, and early visitors to the islands likely embellished the tales of the practice back home. In addition, island tribes themselves may have unwittingly amplified the reputation by spreading rumours about the cannibalism carried out by neighbouring clans to deter Europeans from encroaching further into the islands. As is often the case, within every story lies a grain of truth, but it is invidious to infer any particular localities were responsible for a practice long abandoned.

Subject to volcanic eruptions, earthquakes, cyclones, and tsunamis, the Solomon Islands bear the brunt of mother nature's full arsenal, and journeying to their far western fringe brings a new meaning to the term 'Wild West'. The Solomon Islands' Western Province is a mecca for those with a thirst for adventure. Within the pristine waters punctuated by captivating reefs and uninhabited islands, one of the world's ultimate treks can be experienced.

Life after lava

Climbing the extinct volcano that formed the island of Kolombangara takes several days and offers a challenging ascent to montane cloud forest nearly two thousand metres above the sea below. Trees become unrecognisable nearing the misty summit, encased within layers of mosses, ferns, and epiphytic orchids. As night falls, the remarkable landscape sees the emergence of glowing bioluminescent fungi (*Mycena chlorophos*) and reverberates with the sounds of skittish nightlife. Kolombangara is home to an array of fauna, including rare birds and frogs, poisonous centipedes (*Ethmostigmus rubripes*) growing to over twenty centimetres, and inquisitive mangrove monitors (*Varanus indicus*) among many more island endemics.

Dendrobium spectabile is native to Solomon Islands

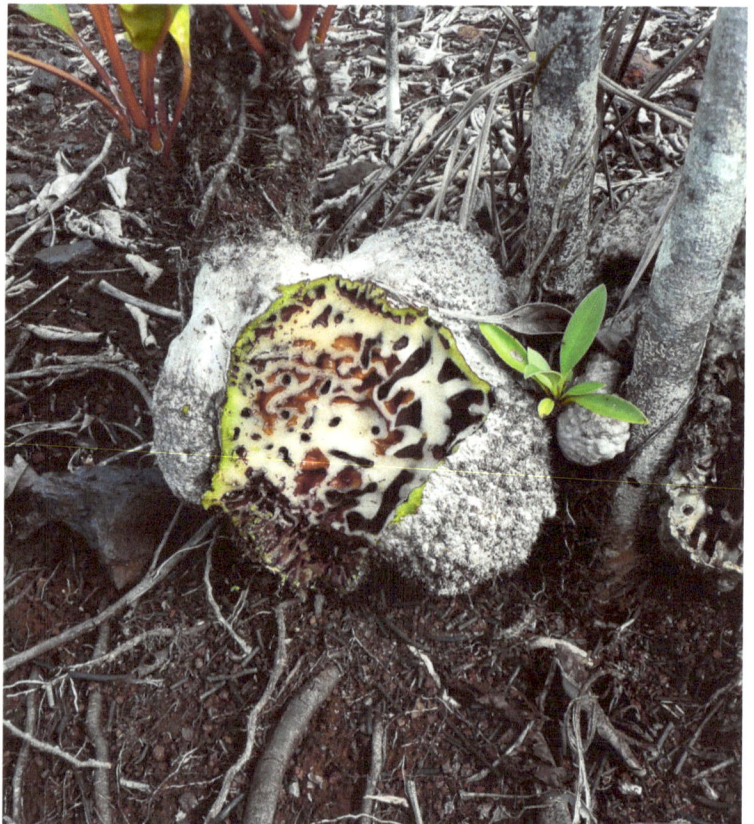

Ant plant (*Myrmecodia tuberosa*)

The island's flora is just as diverse and high in the forest canopy of cloud trees (*Maranthes corymbosa*), a genuine curiosity of horticulture can be found. Epiphytic myrmecophytes, commonly known as 'ant plants', have long discarded the need for soil. Instead, they extract the valuable nutrients they require to survive from another source.

Life is challenging for plants at ground level in the rainforest. The dense canopy cover of the trees above means light is at a premium and hardly adequate for the success of most plants. However, many understory species have evolved traits to deal with this challenge. Some produce huge leaves utilising their surface area to maximise photosynthesis, while others quickly scramble and climb surrounding vegetation vying for a place in the light above.

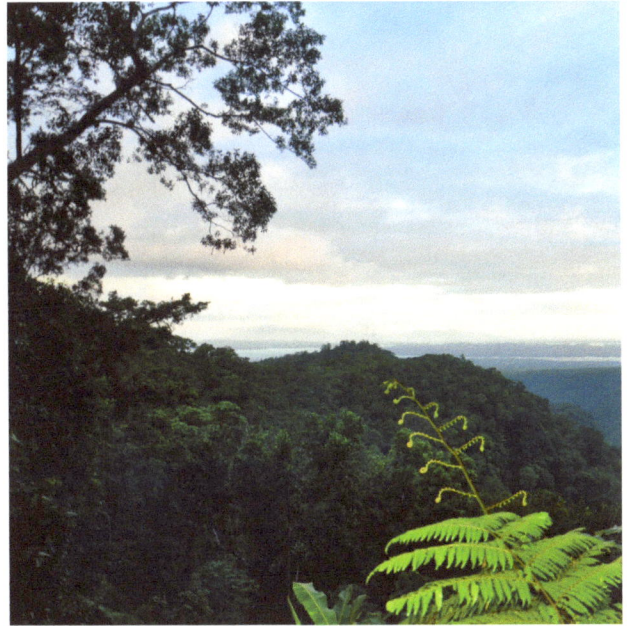

View from Kolombangara cloud forest

Epiphytes have instead evolved so that life takes place basking in the ample sun high up in the canopy of other plants. While this way of life solves the problem of light, it presents challenges of its own. Without access to soil, epiphytes must source nutrition in other ways. Some catch and absorb nutrients from falling debris, while carnivorous epiphytes trap and digest insects and other small animals, but ant plants take advantage of insects more civilly. In a display of ecological mutualism, ant plants have evolved a fleshy stem known as a caudex. This caudex is filled with hollow chambers, which serve as protective nesting spaces for ants.

Mangrove monitor (*Varanus indicus*)

In the tropics, subterranean ants are subjected to heavy rainfall and flooding, while life within the swollen chambers of epiphytic ant plants provides a stable and dry alternative. In return for the accommodation, the ants living within these plants deposit organic nesting materials and digestive waste within the cavities, which break down to provide the plant with a valuable supply of nutrients. In addition, any hungry insect looking to feed on the tissues of an ant plant is likely to regret the decision when greeted by an army of angry ants aggressively defending their home, so this symbiotic relationship makes perfect sense.

Though the range of vegetation in the region is extensive, the native plants of the Solomon Islands are commercially underutilised both within the country and abroad. So, it is a positive development that in recent years projects have been put in place to assist in cataloguing the islands' endemic species. Several countries are now assisting with plant collection and research into the under-investigated floral region. However, it is a slow process in an isolated part of the world, and it is likely the islands are home to many species yet to be discovered.

Unwrapping a culinary mystery

With such a diversity of plants, animals, and culture, it is not surprising that the food in the Solomon Islands follows suit. From mangrove propagules, seaweed, and Pacific cabbage, to an assortment of kumara (sweet potato varieties) and tropical nuts, village cuisine from this part of the world is impossible to replicate elsewhere. Puddings cooked in traditional stone earth ovens are everyday staples and include various ingredients bound together with starchy root crops. The ingredients are mixed and then wrapped in banana leaves before being left to cook in the hot stones.

One pudding, a Western Province specialty, involves folding a paste of crushed island nuts (*Canarium indicum*) between layers of Pacific cabbage (*Abelmoschus manihot*) with delicious results to rival

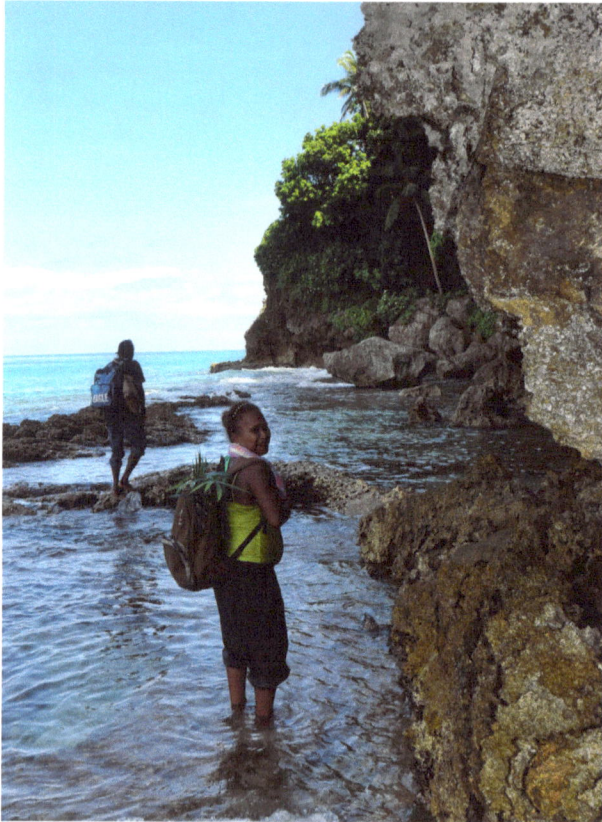

Horticulturists on a plant collection expedition on Bellona

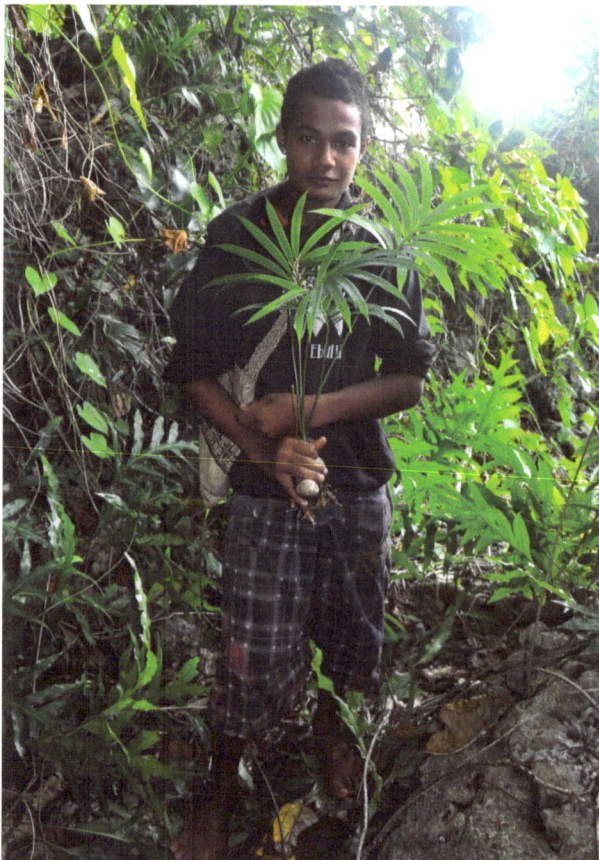

Boy with a sample of *Cycas bougainvilleana*

Pudding made from the local nuts and Pacific cabbage

Shellfish and edible mangrove propagules

even the most reputed of restaurants. Numerous forms of taro are consumed in the country, but which one depends on the soil of the island. Traditional taro (*Colocasia esculenta*) is the preferred crop. However, because it is less able to withstand the poor conditions of saltier coral atolls, other options, including swamp taro (*Cyrtosperma merkusii*), are often cultivated as a substitute.

The vast assortment of sweet potatoes (*Ipomoea batatas*) found throughout Melanesia and the Solomon Islands come in all shapes and sizes, so it is hard to believe they are all variations of the same species. Harder still has been solving the anthropological mystery of how the tuberous vegetable, native to the Americas and Caribbean, made its way to the Pacific islands over a thousand years ago. It has been hypothesised that early Polynesian voyagers may have made it to South America and brought back the material, which was quickly adopted as a cultural staple. However, the extensive genetic diversity in

An island feast including puddings, kumara and various bananas

the crops available across the Pacific seems to point to multiple origins. It has since been suggested that varieties of *I. batatas* may have arrived centuries apart, firstly dispersed by early Polynesian voyagers, before subsequent lineages arrived with Spanish ships and Portuguese traders in the fifteenth and sixteenth centuries CE. Regardless of how it arrived, *I. batatas* has certainly influenced Pacific island culture over the centuries. It is hard to imagine the islands ever being without this humble source of carbohydrates.

Another challenge for anthropologists unique to the Solomon Islands is found in around ten percent of the population and is hard to miss. Many of the dark-skinned Melanesians sport bright blonde hair! Before the advent of genetic mapping, it was thought that this trait might have been passed on and inherited from European explorers or a form of sun bleaching, but recent findings have revealed another explanation. In a fantastic example of convergent evolution, while the gene mutation that caused the blonde pigmentation in Europeans was taking effect in the population between six and ten thousand years ago, a completely different genetic mutation had the same effect in the islands of the South Pacific.

Not your average tender

This trait is particularly prominent in the people of Malaita, the Solomon Islands' most populous province and an area also known for some ingeniously innovative practices, including the minting of 'shell money' and island-building. Nations across Melanesia are renowned for their carving skills. However, the people of Malaita take the practice to a new and intricate level when producing one of the country's traditional forms of currency. Shell money is not used for everyday commerce but is of significant value on occasions where payment is required for a bride or compensation in times of conflict.

Varying in colour from the most valuable red hues to pinks and creams, shell money is made from small pieces of molluscs known as thorny oysters (*Spondylus* spp.). Its production takes place in several

Shell money of Malaita

OFF THE GARDEN PATH

stages. First, the shells are roughly broken into small portions before they are fastened into specially carved slabs of wood and polished with sandstone. The next stage of the process requires meticulous precision. It involves boring a hole in each shell fragment with an ingenious drill comprised of a wooden rod, tipped with a flint-like stone, and manually spun with a fibrous twine. The result is a uniform collection of shell beads ready for a final polish and use for trade.

Creating shell money is a long and tedious process. Still, these aspects have never deterred Malaitans, who are also well known for the creation of around sixty manmade islets across the province's Langa Langa Lagoon. Each one was constructed stone by stone, with families travelling by canoe to dive and collect the submerged building materials before relocating them to shallower reef areas to create the islands, which are now both vegetated and inhabited.

Traditional customs like the use of shell money and payment for a bride are strong in the Solomon Islands. Although there has been much cultural interference over the years, many ancient traditions are still widely upheld. However, one practice unlikely to withstand the test of time involves producing another form of traditional currency. The distinctive red feather money or 'tevau' of the far south eastern province of Temotu is now so rare, it is unlikely to be seen outside of a museum, but it too was once a widely accepted form of currency.

Temotu's red feather money consists of coils of plant fibres, each one decorated with over fifty thousand individual red feathers. The intricate planning involved in creating this unique form of currency is quite bewildering. Skilled bird catchers would use live, tethered birds to lure scarlet honeyeaters (*Myzomela cardinalis*) into traps of sticky plant sap, and once stuck, the birds would be plucked of their vivid plumage. The feathers were then woven into large coils to be stretched, rolled, and used for trade. Each coil could contain the feathers of over three hundred birds and took around seven hundred hours to make, so it is no wonder the practice has not been sustained as successfully as many other island customs.

Life in the capital

Another of the provinces of the Solomon Islands and home to the nation's largest island of the same name is Guadalcanal. Being such a large island, Guadalcanal encompasses beautiful landscapes, waterfalls, and beaches but it is also home to the nation's capital Honiara – a city of stark contrast to the natural beauty of its surrounding island scenery.

An insight into the Solomon Islands, its gardens and gardeners, would be bereft without acknowledging the challenges faced by its people

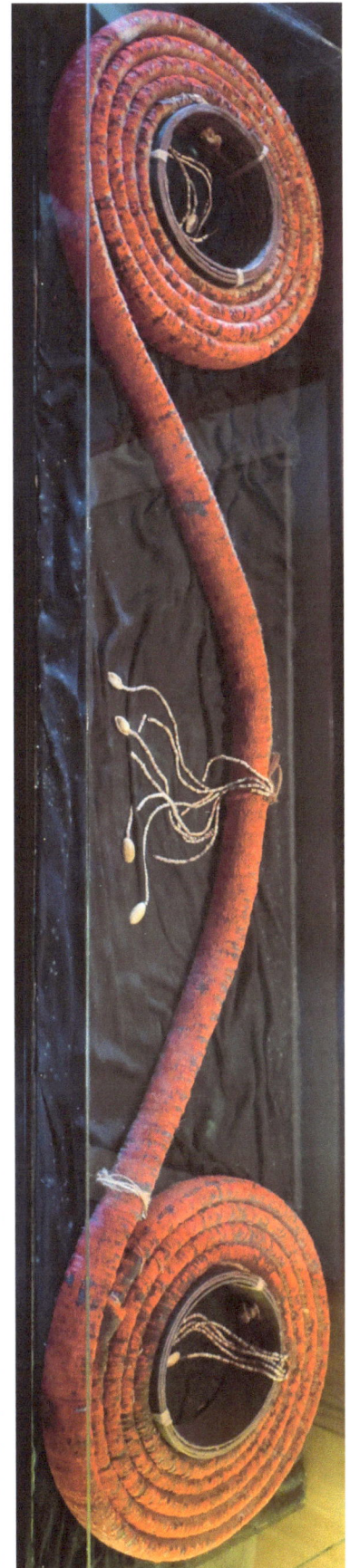

Red feather money of Makira

Tenaru Falls in the rainforest of Guadalcanal

OFF THE GARDEN PATH

both in the country's past and future. In many ways, Honiara displays the culminating results of these challenges. The Solomon Islands have had to bear witness to a history of extensive blackbirding, decades of colonial occupation, civil wars, and some of World War Two's most bloody battles. Frequent natural disasters and continued international exploitation of the country's natural resources also impede the nation's ongoing development, so the fractured society apparent in Honiara is understandable.

A destination for displaced residents hoping for better opportunities than their villages can provide and frequented by hard-living seamen from passing ships, the dusty capital of the Solomon Islands is one reason the country struggles with tourism. It would be fair to assume, at first impression, that amenity horticulture and ornamental gardening are not a priority in this city. Still, with closer observation, clues to a gardening subculture can be found.

From hibiscuses to heliconias, many of the brightly coloured plants which could be expected in a tropical oasis like the Solomon Islands have no natural reason for their occurrence and are certainly not native. They have instead been brought to the Islands over the years and may have quickly disappeared if not carefully fostered at one of several 'mere's gardens' found around the outskirts of Honiara.

Though there are dozens of local dialects in use, the Solomon Islands are united by the Pijin language rather than English, and in Pijin, 'mere' (pronounced Mary) is the word for woman. There are mere's gardens found in Honiara and villages across the country, created and maintained entirely by women. However, the mere's gardens that warrant a place within these pages, as green wonders of the world, are, in fact, best described as nurseries. They are operated by a handful of dedicated women whose interest in ornamental plants and gardening is almost inadvertently driving a cultural change in Honiara.

Example of women at a 'mere's' garden in Honiara

Various forms of croton (*Codiaeum variegatum*)

The women who run these nurseries buy, sell and trade a diverse range of ornamental plants, many of which end up planted across the city. From orchids and palms to ferns, trees, and shrubs, there is a lot to discover when visiting a mere's garden. The gardens allow women to earn an income and sustain healthy livelihoods, but more than that, they have allowed many women the opportunity to become enthusiastic plant collectors and gardeners for their own satisfaction. All the while contributing to building a sense of civic pride in Honiara.

A favourite among the women of the Solomon Islands and highly collectable are crotons (*Codiaeum variegatum*). As the species suggests, *C. variegatum* is astoundingly variable, and there are several hundred cultivated varieties of just this species. The plants are so different in many cases it would be easy to assume they were unrelated, let alone the same species. Possessing leaves that can be anything from oblong, elliptic, or lanceolate to deeply lobed and any combination in between, croton foliage can vary in colour from purples, pinks, and reds to oranges, yellows, and greens, with multiple colours often appearing on a single plant. Native to the Pacific, the plants are an integral component of the tropical charm of the islands of Oceania.

Honiara provides a deceptive façade of horticultural faux pas to visitors, but the women maintaining mere's gardens live a life all about plants. There is no better way to experience the enthusiasm behind the projects than through a visit to the Honiara Central Market early on a Saturday morning. At this market, the true extent and productivity of Guadalcanal's mere's gardens come to light. In a display of floral colour, women bring together a plethora of cut flowers from across the island. From sprays of tiger orchid blooms (*Grammatophyllum speciosum*) to pops of pink torch ginger (*Etlingera elatior*), there is something to suit any taste and enthuse even the blackest thumbed residents.

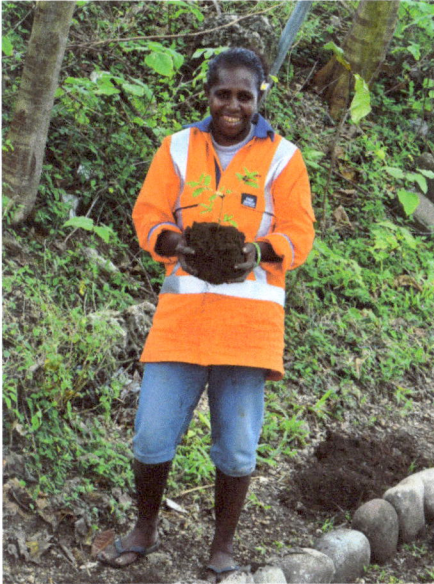
Planting ornamental bed in Honiara

Women processing sweetcorn

Though near the periphery of the city, the tropical rainforest is doing its best to reclaim the roads and reject human intrusion, it has proven almost impossible to green the landscape within Honiara. Store owners see little value in trees, frequently removing them, and the plants that are spared are regularly vandalised. So, the mere gardeners of the country are facing an enormous task trying to impart any kind of cultural change.

Honiara flower market

The greening of Honiara is a mammoth endeavour, but there is no one better to be tasked with the challenge than the women of the Solomon Islands. Hardworking and tenacious, these gardeners are no strangers to adversity. Whether in the house or the field, much of the hard work needed to thrive in the Pacific islands falls to women. Poverty abounds, and the nation's cultural complexity leaves little time to focus on anything else, but still, the mere's gardens persist.

Adversity often breeds kindness and a greater capacity to be happy with the simple things in life. Horticulture also presents these benefits, so it is not surprising that huge smiles are a uniting feature of the women operating mere's gardens. With an affinity to 'stori lelebit' (sit and chat), time passes quickly for women in a mere's garden. The troubles of the city outside are forgotten, lost among the laughter brought on by the inherently cheeky sense of humour unique to Solomon Islands women. Within these gardens, there is a sense of pride, tranquillity, and accomplishment, and changing the culture of Honiara to one that values gardening does not seem so out of reach.

Home to a world of fascinating beauty, the Solomon Islands present extraordinary plants and landscapes but overcoming adversity at every turn, it is the gardeners themselves who are the true wonders of this island nation.

Female horticulturists of the Solomon Islands are driving cultural change

Gardens of Spirituality
Tiger's Nest Monastery
Paro Valley, Bhutan

Centuries hidden in the hills

Settled high amidst cloudy Himalayan peaks and historically closed off to much of the world lies a land of mystery ruled by a lineage of Dragon Kings. A place where the chimes of Buddhist prayer wheels roll across an unbusied landscape and prayer flags dance in the breeze, the Kingdom of Bhutan remains firmly rooted on a path less travelled.

The country possesses one of the world's most dangerous airports - because it is surrounded by mountains and visibility is often poor - but it is not the geography of the location that limits the number of international visitors. The infrequent tourist traffic in the region is the result of strategic planning by the Bhutanese Government to limit the potential impact of tourism on the nation's uniquely unspoiled environment and culture. Until late in the twentieth century, Bhutan existed in isolation, refusing entry to foreign visitors and shying away from the international eye. As a result of its conservative history, the country displays a rare and enchanting cultural authenticity. An authenticity maintained, in part, through a national policy of high value, low impact tourism.

The policy regulates how many tourists reside within Bhutan's borders at any one time by imposing various fees and taxes on travellers. These fees can soar beyond three hundred dollars per day at peak times of the year and undoubtedly dissuade many travellers from considering a visit to the country. It is a somewhat controversial system that has seen Bhutan gain a reputation as a niche destination for the wealthy but ultimately serves its purpose to limit the impact of tourism very effectively.

The Tiger's Nest Monastery, 'Paro Taktsang'

However, Bhutan is well worth a visit and weathering the costs of a short stay, and in reality, the costs are comparable to a European holiday. Most visitors must be accompanied by a pre-booked guide while in the country. As a result, these individuals have become well versed in showcasing the culture and landscape in a very short space of time.

While the landscape and culture of Bhutan receive little international exposure, the country became renowned around the world in the nineteen-seventies when the expression of Gross National Happiness was coined and embraced to measure the country's wealth. Traditionally the term Gross Domestic Product is used to provide a snapshot of a region's economic status and is primarily driven by capitalism, so Gross National Happiness was a radical concept reflective of Bhutan's philosophies for governance.

Gross National Happiness is a concept built on four pillars of sustainable socio-economic development, cultural preservation, environmental conservation, and good governance. Rather than merely considering the monetary value of goods and services to measure wealth, the Gross National Happiness Index indicates the collective happiness and well-being of the population. With the adoption of the philosophy, Bhutan cemented its identity as a free-thinking nation, over time acquiring the image of a Shangrila of spirituality and compassion. It is a valid reputation, and though the country has dark chapters in its past, there is an undeniable air of simplistic happiness and inherent joviality in the population.

With an economic philosophy as unique as Gross National Happiness, it is no surprise that other aspects of Bhutanese society follow suit. From architecture and attire to recreation and cuisine, Bhutan is a nation of distinction. It is an impressive cultural feat given the size and influence of the country's closest neighbours, China and India. The reluctance of the Bhutanese population to stray from tradition has maintained a legitimacy in the region's culture; upheld with such commitment, it was the last nation on Earth to utilise television, only doing so as recently as the cusp of the twenty-first century.

National Museum of Bhutan

With the arrival of technology like television and the internet, it has never been more challenging for the people of Bhutan to resist change, but there are some aspects of life in the region so ingrained they are unlikely to be affected anytime soon. One such aspect is the popularity of the country's national sport – archery.

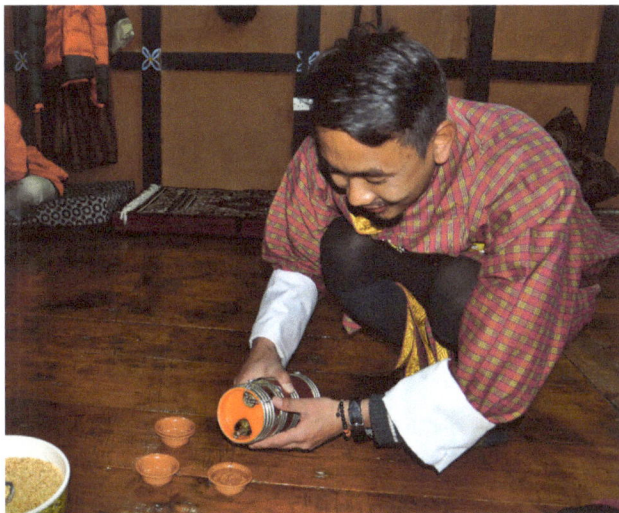
Man pouring traditional alcoholic beverage 'ara'

A national past time treasured by all

For the Bhutanese, archery borders on an obsession. Throughout the nation's history, the bow and arrow have been an essential means of survival during invasions and as tools for hunting. The cultural significance of archery in Bhutan can be observed in many shrines where arrows are often left as offerings. In addition, the weapons play a significant role in several of the region's myths, legends, and religious ceremonies. In modern day Bhutan, archery fields can be found in most villages, where they are an important resource in fostering social interaction, cultural pride, and, more recently, tourism.

Bhutanese archery requires the same concentration and ability as the conventional form of the activity, but it is played as a team sport, using smaller targets over longer distances. Although males traditionally play the sport, the competitions involve entire families in a festive affair that can last days and even weeks before a winning side emerges. Women are active participants in these matches, performing customary

Archery is the national game of Bhutan

Banana bells among other market produce

cheers which take place between archers' shots. In addition, songs written to taunt and unsettle players are enthusiastically sung accompanied by traditional dances in a light-hearted mocking of opposing teams. The archers themselves also engage in verbal exchanges designed to ridicule and distract opponents, and hitting on a meaningful insult is considered as skilful as hitting a bullseye.

Women and children spend days preparing meals and drinks to be consumed throughout the archery competitions. Butter tea made from yaks' butter is a staple, as are various alcoholic beverages which flow from early morning. A favourite is the potent local specialty, ara, made from fermenting or distilling various grains, including rice and maize. Traditionally served warm, it provides an ideal accompaniment to cold winter tournaments and explains the growing cheerfulness seen in participants as the contests unfold. Bhutanese archery goes hand in hand with laughter and smiles, family, and friendship. Integral to the nation's cultural fabric, there is no doubt the sport contributes enormously to the Gross National Happiness of the population.

Dried yak meat or 'yak-sha'

Various forms of dried cheeses are used to flavour Bhutanese cuisine

Abundance at elevation

Alongside archery, food plays an integral role in Bhutanese culture. Meals are a social affair where portions are presented with generosity only matched by variety. The country produces a vast selection of local ingredients, and a visit to any market highlights an array of unusual specialties. Fresh fruit and vegetables are abundant thanks to the country's numerous and varied microclimates. Tropical pawpaws (*Asimina triloba)* and banana bells (*Musa* spp.) sit side by side with temperate summer crops like tomatoes (*Solanum lycopersicum*) and chillies (*Capsicum frutescens*). At the same time, winter crops like cauliflower (*Brassica oleracea* var. *botrytis)* can also be found.

In an age of the 'supermarket', this diversity may seem standard. Fresh produce is now shipped across the world, and out-of-season crops are commonplace on store shelves. However, the cross-seasonal harvests available at the markets of Bhutan are all locally supplied. Existing in seclusion, the country is a picture of self sufficiency, and the diversity in produce on display is a testament to the perseverance of the generations of farmers who have mastered the difficult terrain.

While fresh fruit and vegetables are widely available, a secure supply of valuable protein poses a more significant challenge for people of the Himalayas. Fresh meat and dairy products spoil quickly without refrigeration, and with very few arterial roads, transit within the mountainous landscape is slow and limited. As a result, these products are often dried, ensuring they can be consumed over months without spoiling.

Hanging within homes and the stalls of markets, dried produce including whole fish, and yak meat or 'yak-sha' are common and core to the country's cuisine. Dairy products are also frequently obtained from yaks (*Bos grunniens*) and are used to produce various dried and sometimes fermented cheeses. In the absence of readily available spices, these

Edible cymbidium orchids are found at markets across Bhutan

Dried calendula (*Calendula officinalis*) flowers for export

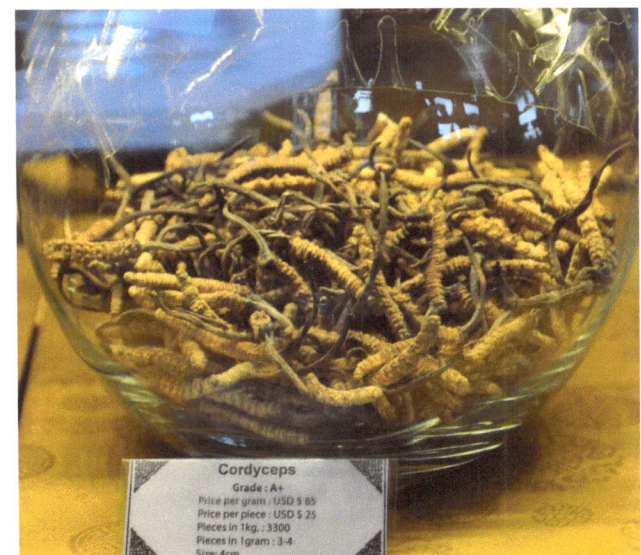
Cordyceps (*Ophiocordyceps sinensis*) for sale

quintessentially Bhutanese delicacies have long been the traditional flavouring element in many meals, paired with copious amounts of chilli and served with rice.

The stalls of Bhutanese markets also exhibit lesser-known culinary specialties. Among them are edible orchid buds from a variety of species including from the well-known ornamental genus *Cymbidium*. Though the edible orchids of Bhutan are only consumed locally, other edible flowers have presented a valuable opportunity for export and economic development in the nation's rural areas in recent years. The tiny farming village of Drachukha is a great example. The village has a population of a little over one hundred inhabitants who have established an exciting co-op of flower growers aiming to supply a niche product to international markets. The farmers grow, harvest, and process their organically grown blooms by hand, resulting in a highly sought-after product valued by innovative chefs and high-end restaurants across the world.

The exotic flower mixes are primarily made using the dried petals of cornflowers (*Centaurea cyanus)* and calendulas (*Calendula officinalis*). Though cornflowers are native to Europe, they have become naturalised in many parts of the world, including Bhutan. Offering edible flowers in shades of blue, through to pink, purple, and white, the blooms maintain a vivid brightness, even after being dried. Calendulas are also foreign and thought to have originated in Europe but have long been cultivated as ornamental garden plants. Their vibrant orange petals are like those of marigolds (*Tagetes* spp.) which are also edible and symbolic for Buddhism in Bhutan, but the petals of calendulas are much easier to harvest and their flavour more palatable. With more than sixty percent of the Bhutanese population residing in similar small mountainous villages and surviving through subsistence farming, this initiative is a promising avenue to support rural economies across the nation.

Classic Bhutanese architecture at Paro Rinphung Dzong

The appeal of organic flower petals popping with colour is almost universal, but the markets of Bhutan harbour another high-value product. A product that is perhaps best considered an acquired taste. *Ophiocordyceps sinensis* is a Himalayan fungi species a world away from the average mushroom. Cordyceps are a group of over four hundred entomopathogenic fungi occurring globally. They are known to parasitise insects, taking over both their minds and bodies before eventually resulting in a gruesome death. *O. sinensis* is a form of cordyceps that is often seen parasitising the larvae of ghost moths (*Thitarodes* spp.). After colonising the insect's body, the reproductive organs of the cordyceps fungus emerge through its hosts mouth, eventually releasing spores and seeking out new victims. Cordyceps fungi have a long history in Eastern medicine and are thought to aid in everything from fighting cancer, diabetes, and inflammation to increasing vitality and youthfulness. In Bhutan, the fungus is harvested and marketed still attached to its host and can sell for over twenty thousand dollars per kilogram.

Preserving the practice of Buddhist architecture

Alongside its national sport and cuisine, there is another aspect of Bhutanese culture unlikely to be affected by the encroachment of globalisation. The country's architecture is as distinct as it is beautiful and, thanks to a recent royal decree, is assured to stay that way. To ensure the nation's buildings maintain their traditional charm, it has been mandated that all buildings must be constructed with multi-coloured wood frontages, small arched windows, and sloping roofs in line with Bhutan's historic customary practices.

Across the country, ancient fortresses known as dzongs and temples display intricately woven carpentry adorning earthen walls. The distinct patterns are also used in domestic dwellings and are seen nowhere else in the world. What makes this Buddhist technique of building even more unique are the

Building face displaying intricately woven carpentry

strict guidelines surrounding the creation of any structures. These rules dictate that no plans can be drawn up, nor are any nails to be used in the construction process.

The extraordinary timber tapestries and natural stone materials add immensely to the atmosphere of Bhutan. Each structure is a handcrafted work of art, but one building is perhaps more famous and frequented than any other.

Perched precariously on a cliff face over eight hundred metres above the Paro Valley below stands the iconic 'Paro Taktsang' or Tiger's Nest Monastery. The legends surrounding the location of the Tiger's Nest began as early as the seventh century CE, when it is believed a holy figure, Guru Padmasambhava, chose to meditate in a natural cave at the location. This event formed a pivotal role in the history of Buddhism in Bhutan and forever secured the sanctity of the site.

In the late seventeenth century, the two-story temple seen today was constructed at the site, but over subsequent centuries succumbed to age-related degradation and a damaging fire. In recent years the temple has been fully restored and now stands in its former glory. The Tiger's Nest is a legendary monastery with a long and colourful history. Offering opportunities for enlightenment accompanied by magnificent views, it has become a standard portion of the itinerary for any visitor when in Bhutan.

A journey to rival the destination

A visit to the Tiger's Nest involves several hours of steep trekking that provides an ideal opportunity to take in another aspect of the landscape core to the country's character. The flora of Bhutan varies from commanding trees and flamboyant shrubs to vigorous climbers and fleeting annual herbs. The Bhutan cypress (*Cupressus torolusa*) is the national tree of the country. The species has religious significance, and as a result, the trees are often seen growing near temples and monasteries but can be found in abundance across the region. The Bhutan cypress can grow to forty metres in height. First growing in a dense conical form, the trees mature to develop a majestic weeping habit and provide a valuable source of timber. Like many conifers, the species is also a source of important essential oils used medicinally and in cosmetics.

Accompanying the Bhutan cypress in the hills of the Paro Valley are vast stands of an even more prevalent coniferous species. The Himalayan blue pine (*Pinus wallichiana*) is widespread and forests

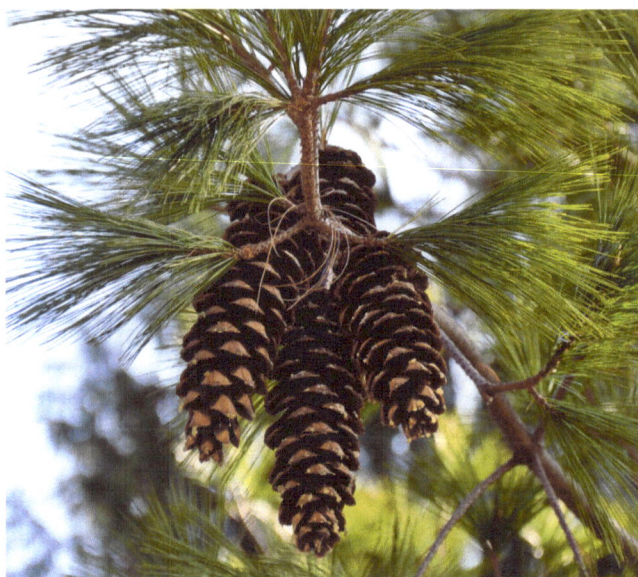

Cones of the Himalayan blue pine *(Pinus wallichiana)*

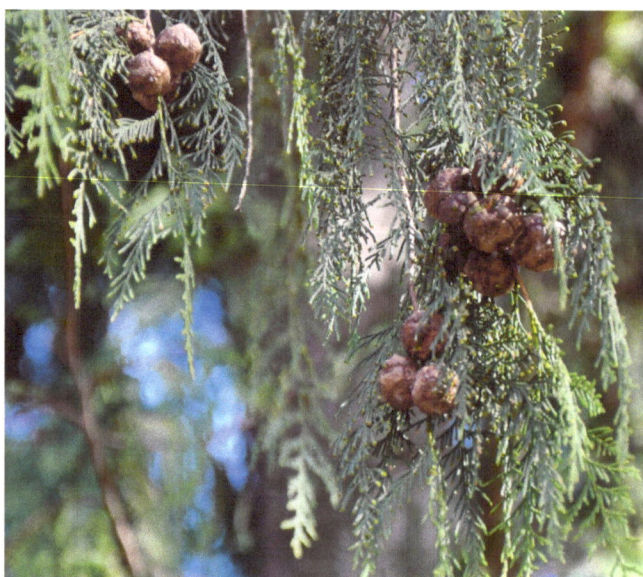

Cones of and foliage Himalayan cypress *(Cupressus torolusa)*

dominated by the species span more than one hundred thousand hectares of the Bhutanese landscape, including the sheer cliff faces leading to the Tiger's Nest Monastery. The trees provide durable timber but are better known as a commercial source for the household solvent turpentine, distilled from the abundant natural resin produced by the species.

P. wallichiana is widespread across mountainous regions from eastern Afghanistan to China, but its closely related cousin, the Bhutan white pine (*Pinus bhutanica*), is considerably more restricted. This species is almost endemic to Bhutan, though its distribution extends slightly across the country's borders into neighbouring China and India. *P. bhutanica* was initially described around the time that Bhutan first opened its borders to international visitors, but it was long considered to be just another variety of *P. wallichiana* and has only recently been accepted as a unique *Pinus* species.

Changes in botanical nomenclature like that of *P. wallichiana* are becoming a common occurrence as technology advances across the globe. Traditionally, plants have been grouped into families and genera based on their appearance, but with the development of genomic sequencing, botanists can now determine how closely plants are genetically related, which has uncovered some surprising findings. Many plants that look similar and have traditionally been considered to be related have proven to be far less akin than first thought, while other plants that display few visual similarities are revealing they are closer relatives than anyone could have guessed from appearance alone. In light of the emerging data, plants are increasingly being pulled from one family to another and acquiring new names as a result.

The effects of unstable nomenclature are widespread across the world and contribute to the frustration of many a gardener. In Bhutan, even the nation's national flower has fallen victim to a recent

Himalayan cypress silhouette against Paro Valley

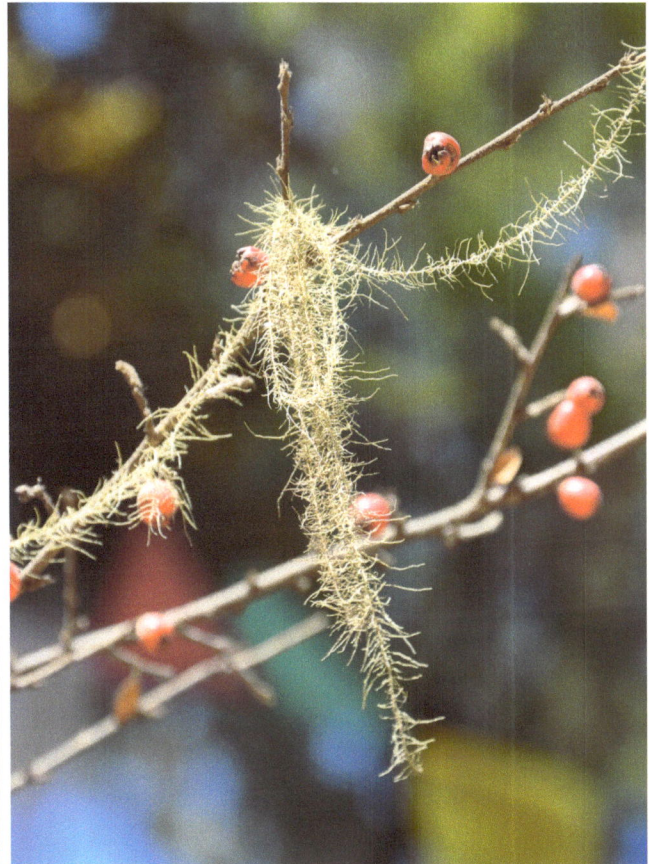

Usnea, a type of lichen hangs from trees along the trek

title change. The Himalayan blue poppy was once thought to be a singular species named *Meconopsis grandis* and found throughout the Himalayas. The stunning blue flowers made the sample discovered in Bhutan in the nineteen-thirties an ideal choice for the country's floral emblem. However, over the years, many variations have been observed in the *Meconopsis* genus resulting in numerous new species being described. Many species within the genus freely hybridise, and some botanists believe that several plants that have been named new species are variants of just a handful of true species. As a result, many names are currently unresolved on the global stage. Nevertheless, it was recently announced that the national flower of Bhutan was misidentified all those years ago and was not *M. grandis* at all but rather a new species, *M. gakyidiana*. Regardless of its scientific name, there is no arguing that the exotic beauty of the blue poppy makes it a fitting choice to represent Bhutan.

Adding to the mystical atmosphere of the ascent to the Tiger's Nest are the masses of lichen species hanging from the branches of the trees found along the route. Easily confused as Spanish moss (*Tillandsia usneoides*), an unusual epiphytic plant species, lichens result from a symbiotic relationship between species of algae or cyanobacteria and fungi. The algae produce food through photosynthesis in a mutually beneficial arrangement, while the fungal organisms provide surface area and structural protection. The relationship has proven so successful that lichens can be found growing just about anywhere from the surfaces of wood, rocks, and soil to hanging in mid-air. Lichens are often considered an indicator of environmental health, and their prevalence in the region supports the idea that Bhutan is a paradise in the clouds.

The Tiger's Nest Monastery seems to defy the laws of physics

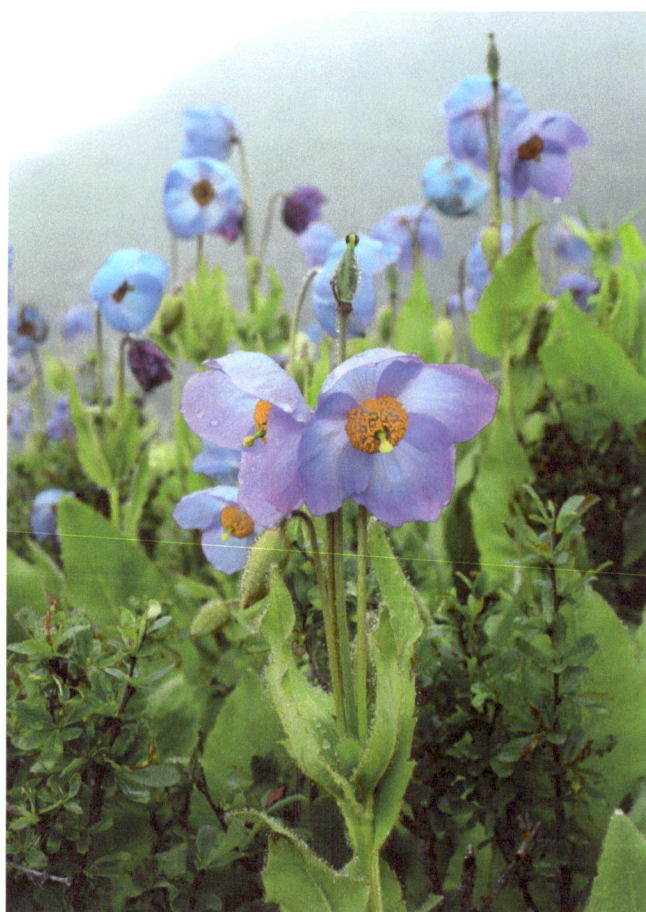

Bhutan's national flower *Meconopsis gakyidiana*

Opportunities for horticultural enlightenment

The Tiger's Nest Monastery is just one of many religious sites in Bhutan that share a common theme. Monasteries and temples in the country exhibit a unique form of gardening in the short-lived floral colour that is presented to Buddha each day. Continually renewed as flowers fade, no two displays are ever the same, giving these gardens of spirituality a distinct ephemeral quality. The short-lived scenes are made more elusive because photography in the locations is rarely allowed. The rules around photography in temples are in place to ensure the religious significance of the sites is respected but serve a dual purpose, as they allow visitors to fully appreciate the fleeting scenes.

Cut flowers sit side by side with glowing butter lamps, brightly coloured textiles, and religious figures but these gardens are beyond mere flower arrangements. Permanent plantings in ornately presented pots also feature in the scenery. Species of ivy, including Bhutan's native Himalayan ivy (*Hedera nepalensis)*, are common, as are azaleas (*Azalea* spp.), roses (*Rosa* spp.), and dahlias (*Dahlia* spp.) The pots are carefully tended and hand-watered by devout monks who moonlight as gardeners.

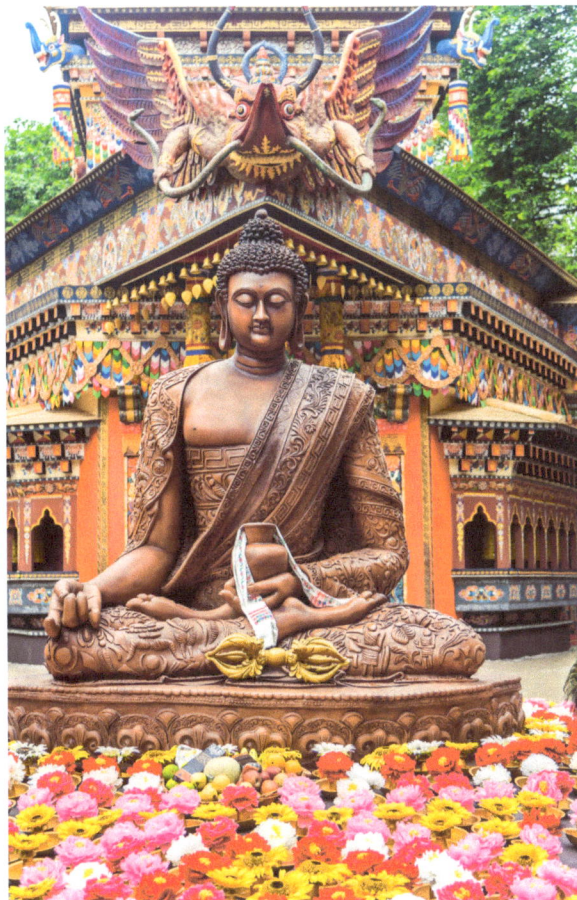

Floral offering are a unique form of fleeting gardens

Ornately potted ivy and azaleas

In some locations where soil is available, small trees, including calamondins (*Citrus × microcarpa*) and camellias (*Camellia* spp.), are incorporated into the landscape in a gardening recipe that can only be described as uniquely Bhutanese.

From its temples and monasteries to its food and traditions, Bhutan is a nation unlike any other. The region is portrayed as a mountainous realm where the air is clean, the festivities run long, and the people are happy. For the most part, this is true, and why wouldn't it be? The landscape is idyllic, many of the harmful elements of globalisation have been kept at bay, and deep-rooted cultural traditions remain intact. These aspects alone justify a spot for Bhutan's evanescent gardens to stand among the world's green wonders; the fantastic display of unusual plants found in the region just provides the icing on the horticultural cake.

Bhutan's largest Buddha stands over fifty metres tall

The Pinnacle of Horticulture
Gardens by the Bay
Marina South, Singapore

A serve of horticulture with all the trimmings

As an epicentre for global trade and transit, Singapore strives to provide an ever-evolving tapestry of offerings to enthral international visitors. Travellers need only to take their first steps into the country's airport, and it becomes clear that horticulture plays a significant role in this pursuit. The famed Changi International Airport offers much more than a thumb-twiddling layover for the thousands of global commuters who pass through its gates each day. Instead, thanks to a floristic transformation, the destination is now highly sought after and far from a tedious interruption to greater journeys.

Alongside mouth-watering food and shopping malls, horticulture is given pride of place within the complex, where a multitude of themed gardens are on display. From a cacti-covered rooftop to an enchanting orchidarium, there is even a butterfly garden used to raise and showcase thousands of the brightly coloured insects. The standard in gardening set within Changi Airport is a fitting precursor as to what can be expected across the rest of Singapore, where amazingly, this standard is not just met, it is far exceeded.

The horticulturists and landscape architects involved in creating Singapore's streetscapes demonstrate an unrivalled triumph in urban greening, particularly regarding vertical gardening and green architecture. Whether it is the inclusion of plants in verges or on the surfaces of the city's concrete canopy, Singapore deserves its reputation as a garden nation. So, with such high horticultural standards commonplace, how does a country like Singapore freshen up its botanical palette? The answer is by creating one of the most ambitious and well-executed gardens the world has ever seen.

Aerial view of Gardens by the Bay

Waterfalls within the Serene Garden

Extraordinary is an understatement when describing Singapore's Gardens by the Bay, which opened to the world in June of two thousand and twelve. The extensive site is divided into three substantial sections – Bay South, Bay East, and Bay Central – which, in total, span over one hundred hectares of land. When considering the enormity of this display of cutting-edge horticulture and its mastery over the natural environment, it is evident that preparations must have begun far earlier than the public opening. In fact, the concept of the gardens was first announced in two thousand and five, before construction works commenced over subsequent years.

Transformed from concept to reality in just seven years, a visit to the gardens begs the question; how can any landscape look so healthy and established in such a short space of time? The answer lies with a multidisciplinary team of professionals, from horticulturists to engineers, who contributed to the realisation of the Gardens by the Bay. Early in the project's planning phase, decisions were made to source and utilise as many advanced trees as possible to be included among fast-growing species suited to Singapore's tropical climate. Many established plants, including several mature frangipanis (*Plumeria rubra*) were rescued from construction sites. While others which included towering Chilean wine palms (*Jubaea chilensis*) and majestic African boabs (*Adansonia digitata*), were sourced from

Minimalist themes in the Serene Garden inspired by the Japanese concept of Zen

an eclectic mix of domestic sites from around the world. Many specimens are rare and even include gargantuan ancient olives (*Olea europaea*) thought to be over one thousand years old.

In addition to sourcing and utilising mature plants to create the illusion of a long-established garden, Singapore's tropical climate provided the horticulturists behind the Gardens by the Bay an ideal environment to establish and multiply plants quickly. A range of strategies were utilised to expedite plant growth, from rooting propagation material directly into garden beds to casting pruning refuse over any bare patches of earth, knowing it would likely take root and form new plants - the gardens were able to go from bare to there with great efficiency.

Over fifty million visitors have passed through the gates at the Gardens by the Bay, and it is not surprising. The site presents a fantastic day out, and for gardeners, it has to be seen to be believed.

Ficus microcarpa **topiaries seen in Bay South**

Section of the Heritage Gardens

Giant structures filled with thousands of individual plants at the Supertree Grove

Floral Fantasy exhibition

Amenity gardens delivered on a scale like never before

Set amidst expansive lawns and offering tranquil views of Singapore's Marina Bay skyline, the rolling open space of the Bay East section of the gardens is enjoyed by locals and international visitors alike. Offering numerous pavilions and event spaces, including the 'Meadow' - a favourite setting for open-air concerts, Bay East provides a peaceful and relaxing escape from the surrounding city. Linking the larger sections, Bay Central is the smallest and least established portion of the Gardens by the Bay landscape but retains great potential for future development in years to come.

While both the Bay East and Bay Central areas provide beautiful leisure space, immaculate parklands and add to the overall scale of the Gardens by the Bay, these areas are somewhat pedestrian compared to the spectacles of horticultural excellence offered to guests in the Bay South area. Incorporating cutting-edge technology, specialised greenhouses stand alongside themed gardens, lakes, and a plethora of sculptural hardscaping. The Bay South area of the Gardens by the Bay is a true wonder of the horticultural world.

The open-air gardens of Bay South offer a range of landscapes. The 'Canyon' showcases several hundred species of arid zone plants alongside huge naturally formed and ancient white boulders brought from Shandong in China. The 'Serene Garden' is inspired by the minimalist concept of Japanese Zen gardens. In the 'Heritage Gardens', visitors are taken through the important plants of Singapore's main ethnic groups, including plants intrinsically linked to the Indian, Chinese, and Malay cultures. True to Singapore's history, there is even a colonial section featuring commercial crops introduced to the region.

Ancient boulders of The Canyon

OFF THE GARDEN PATH

The 'World of Plants' section of Bay South contains a collection of informative gardens showcasing the biological relationships of plants in the natural world. A window into the evolution of plants is displayed within the space, where specific sections highlight everything from the importance of biodiversity, to plant adaptations and the unique commonalities within plant families. Other areas have been established to emphasise the significance of pollinator relationships in plant reproduction. If visitors have enough time, the engaging display continues to enthuse, with further sections established to provide sensory insights into the influence of fungi in maintaining healthy plant communities.

The Gardens by the Bay become a neon wonderland

Gardens by the Bay's World of Plants also consists of an impressive collection of gigantic topiaries, including animals and insects involved in unique relationships with Singapore's plants. The gargantuan sculptures have been created using Chinese banyan figs (*Ficus microcarpa*), a fast-growing and small-leaved fig ideal for topiary. While the giant figures now stand flawlessly in the Bay South grounds, their initial production took place abroad and in several stages. The topiaries are so large they were first grown in sections in Vietnam using many plants for each segment before being brought to the site and fashioned into their final forms. Once constructed at Gardens by the Bay, the sections were given time to grow together and produce the faultless specimens on display today.

Days and nights offer two completely different experiences

Other sections of Bay South include the 'Floral Fantasy' display, an ever-changing, immersive, botanical extravaganza, and the 'Sun Pavilion', which is comprised of over one hundred desert-dwelling plant species. Far beyond the pedestrian, the enticements of Bay South are extraordinary feats in horticulture. Still, for all the horticultural merit mentioned thus far, there are brighter jewels in the Gardens by the Bay crown. Botanical jewels unlike anything else in the world.

Gems in a horticultural crown

Ensuring no guest leaves without their horticultural stomach full, the Gardens by the Bay are also home to the 'Supertree Grove', a garden installation where the lines between hard and soft landscape features are challenged on an unprecedented scale. In traditional landscaping, hard features are the elements in a garden that are not alive, while plants are regarded as soft features and make up the living aspect of an area, but the Supertree Grove is somehow both. In this section of the gardens, massive tree-like steel columns tower thirty-five, forty, and even fifty meters above the surrounding grounds. However, although the supertree scaffolds are steel, they have been creatively adorned with diverse plant species. Encompassing brightly coloured bromeliads, lush ferns, and vigorous climbers, it is hard to decipher where steel ends and plants begin.

The attraction is a masterpiece of landscape design, but pioneering installations like the Supertree Grove come with uncharted maintenance requirements. Winding atop the commanding structures, a canopy walk offers visitors an impressive view of the surrounding cityscape. It is also a valuable perch for the gardeners tasked with caring for the plants at such vertiginous heights. Though the canopy walk is advantageous for staff undertaking maintenance of the vertical gardens, it does not provide access to all the plants housed in the towers. Under the cover of darkness, when the gardens' gates have closed, access to the harder to reach sections of the grove is instead achieved utilising heavy machinery and mechanical lifts in what is quite literally 'next level' gardening.

Singapore's iconic conservatories

Nightly lightshow held at the Supertree Grove

As night falls in Singapore, the Gardens by the Bay provide a completely different encounter for patrons than that which would have been experienced just a few hours before. Suddenly alight with the enchanting glow of hundreds of thousands of neon lights, the gardens are transformed into a botanical wonderland guaranteed to impress. The centrepiece of the luminous festivities is a nightly light show within the Supertree Grove. With the intensity of the tropical heat relenting with the setting sun, the show is a great way to round out a day of horticultural adventure.

Within these grounds, guests can expect to find each attraction more spellbinding than the last. Even the Supertree Grove is rivalled in its horticultural decadence compared with the two biggest drawcards of the site. The futuristic greenhouses now synonymous with the Singapore skyline and the gardens within them are undoubtedly the crowning glory of Gardens by the Bay.

A botanical wonderland in the clouds

While they may appear similar on the outside, each of the two cutting-edge greenhouses at the Gardens by the Bay serve a unique purpose. Both houses are designed to allow the gardens' horticulturists to grow and display a range of plants otherwise unsuited to Singapore's tropical climate, but the environmental conditions achieved within each structure are completely different. The smaller of the two installations has been named the 'Cloud Forest' and houses climate specialised plant species of the world's tropical montane cloud forests. The second structure is known as the 'Flower Dome'. It plays host to a diverse collection of species from areas including the Americas, Mediterranean, South Africa and even Australia.

View from the top of the Cloud Forest Conservatory

Whether guests have finished venturing through the vast outdoor areas or are looking for somewhere to rest until the nightly Supertree light show, these climate-controlled structures provide an unlikely opportunity for respite from the surrounding tropical heat. In contrast to the warm, humidifying effect achieved in a traditional glasshouse, visitors are presented with a cool and refreshing breeze when entering these examples of technological innovation.

Beyond the entranceway to the Cloud Forest stands a commanding waterfall flowing from a mountainous vertical garden and delivering an impact that sets the standard for a truly unique experience. Numerous walkways embedded throughout the multistorey construction allow visitors to wander through the elevated plantings to explore the diverse species on offer. Natural montane cloud forests are found from between one thousand and four thousand metres above sea level, and accessing them

The ultimate vertical gardening is found in the Cloud Forest

often involves days of trekking to isolated parts of the planet, but at Gardens by the Bay, sophisticated climate control systems replicate the environmental conditions perfectly.

This technology ensures the extensive collection of intricate plantings is at its best year-round and adds to the immersive experience for visitors. A thick mist provides a surreal feeling of walking among the clouds and has the benefit of promoting a natural supply of moss on any exposed surfaces, adding to the authenticity of the entire installation. To facilitate the success of the Cloud Forest during its inception, the mountainous centrepiece was covered with a special mix of cement and organic material. This material acts in place of soil, and being porous, allows water and nutrients to be easily absorbed by the plants growing on it.

The Cloud Forest greenhouse is a playground for fans of epiphytes, rare and unusual orchids, pitcher plants, and bromeliads but growing plants away from

Rare orchid display

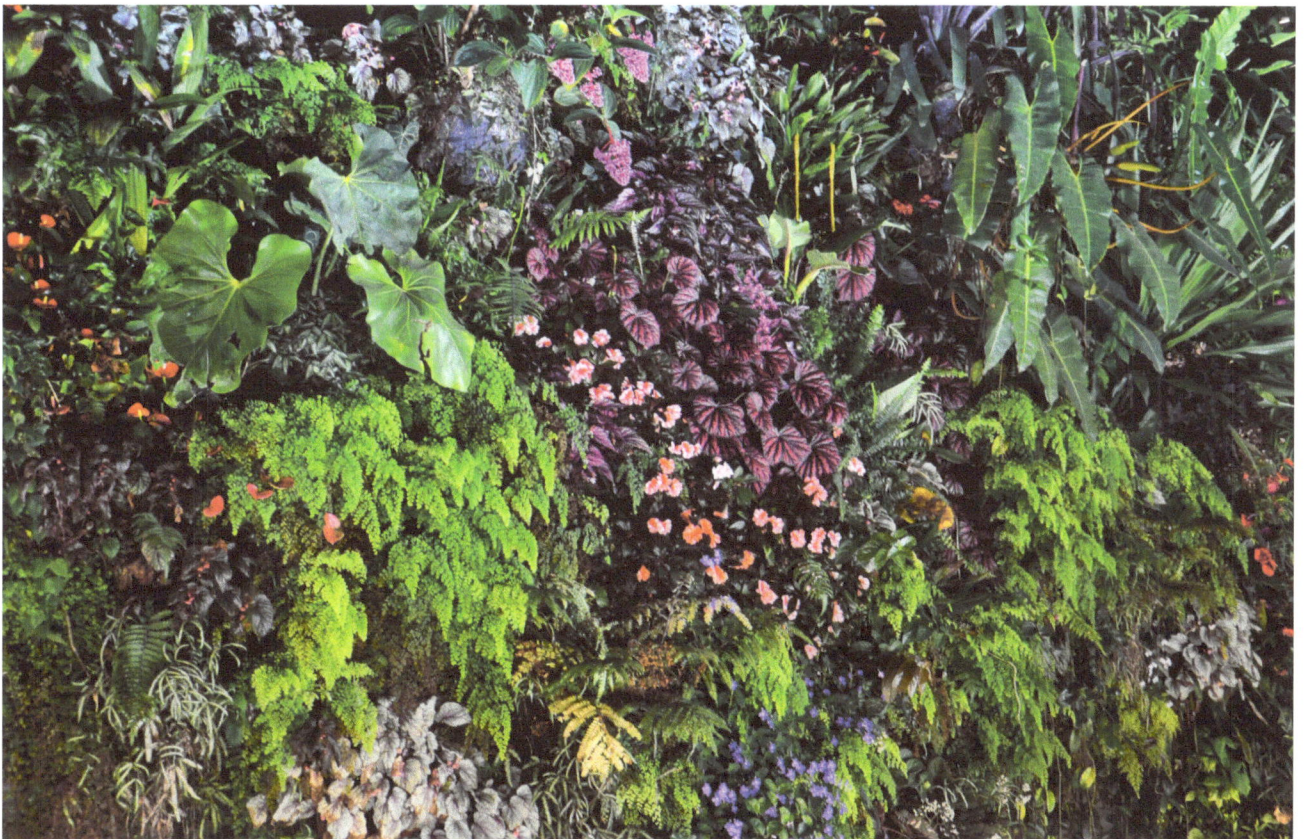

An illustration of the diversity of plants fostered within the Cloud Forest

Displays at Gardens by the Bay are constantly changing

Ancient olive thought to be over one thousand years old

their natural climate is not without its challenges. Some plants are growing far from the beneficial insects that exist in the wild to control the pests and diseases likely to target them. Plants may also be exposed to entirely new pests and diseases. As is the case in any garden, when a pest or disease attack does occur, the Gardens by the Bay horticulturalists need to apply appropriate controls. However, with all maintenance timed to occur after hours, visitors are always guaranteed a perfectly executed interpretation of what would be experienced walking in a real cloud forest.

'Blossom Beats' display within the Flower Dome

A short stroll away from the Cloud Forest, doors open to the Flower Dome, which holds the record of the world's largest glass greenhouse. It is hard to fathom how the people behind the botanical palette have managed to achieve such a complicated feat of horticulture within the structure. The plants growing in the Flower Dome are as diverse in their needs as they are in their habits and forms.

While most of the species on display are reasonably hardy and suited to temperate climates, the challenge of growing plants in a completely synthesised environment extends beyond the above-ground conditions and into the soil. Many of the plants exhibited arrived at the gardens fully established, which meant that the planning that went into creating soil profiles of varying depths and compositions had to be incredibly precise. In addition, during the planning and realisation of the Flower Dome, designers had to predict and account for what impacts any additional canopy cover from arriving tree specimens would have on existing plantings.

It is a credit to everyone involved that this foresight and contingency planning has resulted in the thriving scene within the Flower Dome today. The conservatory houses everything from giant bottle trees, olives, and palms, to established grass trees (*Xanthorrhoea glauca*), cloud pruned Leyland cypress (*Cupressus* x *leylandii*), and impressive cacti, including species of *Pilocereus* and *Echinocactus*. Growing in synergy in the tropical climate of Singapore, the plant diversity within this greenhouse is an illustration of the Gardens by the Bay's technological triumph over the outside environment.

Hidden within the immense floral façade of the Gardens by the Bay exist the industrial hubs that bolster the gardens' success. These include the technology-driven facilities that allow for the extensive

View inside the Flower Dome

climate manipulation required in the Cloud Forest and Flower Dome greenhouses. Far from anything resembling conventional air conditioning, before any outside air can enter the greenhouses, it is stripped of moisture in a process using lithium chloride. It is then cooled by industrial chillers powered by an environmentally conscious process that utilises the region's horticultural waste as an energy source. Unwanted fluctuations in temperature within the greenhouses are also reduced by a unique glass that decreases the heat energy allowed into the glasshouse while maintaining the levels of light required by the sun-loving plants below.

Singapore's Gardens by the Bay illustrate what can be achieved when technological advancement is combined with a deep-seated affinity with plants. In a never-ending pursuit of excellence, the Gardens by the Bay are constantly evolving, ensuring no two visits are ever the same. No expense was spared during the creation of the site. With close to four hundred staff involved in its day-to-day operation, this gardening phenomenon is poised to continue to set the highest of horticultural standards well into the future and inspire many generations to come.

Gardens by the Bay at dusk

Return to the Garden Path
(Epilogue)

The world is an amazing place that can change in an instant. The gardens explored within these pages may seem out of reach for a time, but visiting such sites has never been an easy journey, and while the rapid changes we continue to experience can be unnerving, plants offer silent counsel. Brainless but intelligent, they remain unaffected by trivial matters on their paths to fruition, free of emotion and wise with their resources. They existed across the planet well before the arrival of humans and will likely persist well after we depart. Plants are able to adapt and survive in the face of extraordinary challenges; clearly, we need them more than they need us.

From the most ancient of algae to the highly evolved angiosperms of today, across the planet, the plants we perceive as passive and inconsequential have been writing the script for the success of the human race. Some have fallen, allowing civilisations to thrive. Others have lived through the ages, witnessing the rise and collapse of empires. More, undoubtedly, exist in obscurity, still to be discovered, but may yet influence future generations.

Plants have the power to build, change and enhance cultures, and while humans have long exploited these organisms, they too have manipulated us in a perpetual battle for survival. Farming is a perfect example. As humans have been mastering agriculture, the crops grown have quietly brokered deals that ensure these species will thrive for at least as long as our species does.

Regardless of how we define them, in the battle for survival fought by all living things, gardens in all their forms are the ultimate demonstration of biological mutualism. Plants provide a diversity of benefits, and it is the role of a gardener to return the favour.

Journeying off the garden path presents the opportunity to experience some of the planet's most extraordinary interpretations of gardening. However, you do not need to travel the globe to see the world's green wonders - they start in your own backyard.

References and Further Reading

Chapter 1: Bangladesh

Anni, Afroza Zaman. 2020. 'Shitol Pati: A Heritage on the Verge of Extinction'. *The Daily Sun*. Retrieved July 11, 2021 (https://www.daily-sun.com/printversion/details/460062/Shitol-Pati:-A-Heritage-On-The-Verge-Of-Extinction-).

Backyard Brains. n.d. 'Sensitive Mimosa Pudica Electrophysiology'. Retrieved July 11, 2021 (https://backyardbrains.com/experiments/Plants_SensitiveMimosaPudica).

Bbarta24. 2017. 'UNESCO Recognises "Shitol Pati" as Intangible Cultural Heritage'. Retrieved July 11, 2021 (http://en.bbarta24.net/national/2017/12/06/14423).

Bhattacharjee, Atanu, Shastry Chakrakodi Shashidhara and Santanu Saha. 2015. 'Nootropic Activity of Crataeva Nurvala Buch-Ham Against Scopolamine Induced Cognitive Impairment'. *EXCLI Journal* (14): 335-345. doi: 10.17179/excli2014-541.

Choudhury, Junaid K., Shekhar R. Biswas, M. Sazedul Islam, Oliur Rahman and Sadar Nasir Uddin. 2004. *Biodiversity of Ratargul Swamp Forest, Sylhet*. Bangladesh: The World Conservation Union. Retrieved July 11, 2021 (https://portals.iucn.org/library/sites/library/files/documents/2004-083-3.pdf).

Gilman, Sharon. 1999. "Plant Adaptations". Course Notes, Coastal Carolina University, Conway, SC. Retrieved July 13, 2021 (https://ci.coastal.edu/~sgilman/778Plants.htm). 9(3): 1-7, 2019; Article no.ARJASS.48592 ISSN: 2456-4761

Kazi Moriom Jahan and Afm Zakaria. 2019 'Environmental Movement and the Conservation of Forest: A Case Study on Ratargul Swamp Forest of Sylhet, Bangladesh'. Asian Research Journal of Arts & Social Sciences. Retrieved 12 July, 2021. (https://www.researchgate.net/publication/335527212_Environmental_Movement_and_the_Conservation_of_Forest_A_Case_Study_on_Ratargul_Swamp_Forest_of_Sylhet_Bangladesh)

Khan, Mobarak Hossain, Wakil Ahmed and Momen Chowdhury. 2021. 'Musical Instruments'. *Banglapedia: National Encyclopedia of Bangladesh*. Retrieved July 12, 2021 (http://en.banglapedia.org/index.php?title=Musical_Instruments).

Mondal, Badal Kumar. 2020. 'A Study of Ratargul Swamp Forest, Bangladesh'. *Green Page*. Retrieved July 11, 2021 (https://thegreenpagebd.com/a-study-of-ratargul-swamp-forest-bangladesh-2/).

Smriti, Saifun Nahar. n.d. 'Ratargul Swamp Forest: The Green Mystery and Discussion of Plants (Part 2)'. *Plantlet*. Retrieved July 11, 2021 (https://plantlet.org/ratargul-swamp-forest-the-green-mystery-discussion-of-plants-part-2/).

The Nations Online Project. n.d. 'Bangladesh'. Retrieved July 11, 2021 (https://www.nationsonline.org/oneworld/bangladesh.htm).

Titcumb, Mary. 2005. *Swampy Riparian Woodland*. Victoria: Department of Sustainability and the Environment. Retrieved July 11, 2021 (https://www.gbcma.vic.gov.au/downloads/EVCs/SwampyRiparianWoodland.pdf)

USAID's Climate-Resilient Ecosystems and Livelihoods (CREL) Project. 2015. "Newsletter, July 2015". Retrieved July 13, 2021 (https://nishorgo.org/wp-content/uploads/2017/03/2015_07_E-NewsLetter.pdf).

Weather Online. n.d. 'Bangladesh'. Retrieved July 11, 2021 (https://www.weatheronline.co.uk/reports/climate/Bangladesh.htm).

Chapter: 2 Jordan

Brandes, Dietmar. 2010. *Synanthropic Flora of Petra (Jordan)*. Technische Universität Braunschweig. Braunschweig: Digitale Bibliothek. Retrieved July 12, 2021 (https://www.researchgate.net/publication/257364214_Synanthropic_flora_of_Petra_Jordan).

Greening the Desert Project. n.d. Retrieved July 13, 2021 (https://www.greeningthedesertproject.org/).

Henry, Donald and Rosa Maria Albert. 2004. 'Herding and Agricultural Activities at the Early Neolithic Site of Ayn Abū Nukhayla (Wadi Rum, Jordan). The Results of Phytolith and Spherulite Analyses'. *Paléorient* 30(2): 81-92. doi: 10.3406/paleo.2004.1012.

Lingis, Alphonso. 2002. 'Petra'. *Journal of Visual Culture* 1(1): 47-45. doi:10.1177/147041290200100104

Whitman, Elizabeth. 2019. 'A Land Without Water: The Scramble to Stop Jordan from Running Dry'. *Nature*, September 4. Retrieved July 12, 2021 (https://www.nature.com/articles/d41586-019-02600-w).

Chapter 3: Turkey

Encyclopedia Britannica. 2019. 'Cappadocia'. Retrieved July 12, 2021 (https://www.britannica.com/place/Cappadocia).

Ercisli, Sezal. 2009. 'Apricot Culture in Turkey'. *Scientific Research and Essays* 4 (8). Retrieved July 12, 2021 (https://www.researchgate.net/publication/228620079_Apricot_culture_in_Turkey).

Kayakapi Premium Caves. n.d. 'Cappadocia'. Retrieved July 12, 2021 (https://www.kayakapi.com/cappadocia).

Ozkan, Burhan and Aziz Ozmeri. 2002. 'An Overview of Turkish Agriculture'. Paper presented at the International Workshop on Conservation Agriculture for Sustainable Wheat Production in Rotation with Cotton in Limited Water Resource Areas, January. Tashkent, Uzbekistan. Retrieved July 12, 2021 (https://www.researchgate.net/publication/295074948_An_Overview_of_Turkish_Agriculture).

Ozkan, Gulay, Senem Kamiloglu, Tugba Ozdal, Dilek Boyacioglu and Esra Capanoglu. 2016. 'Potential Use of Turkish Medicinal Plants in the Treatment of Various Diseases'. *Molecules* 21 (3): 257. doi: 10.3390/molecules21030257.

Turgay, Ozlem and Inci Cinar. 2017. 'Salep: The Name of the Plant, Powder, Hot Beverage, Food Ingredient'. *Kahramanmaras Sutcu Imam University Journal of Engineering Sciences* 20 (3): 68-71. doi: 10.17780/ksujes.341382.

Chapter 4: Myanmar

Charney, Michael W. 2015. *A History of Modern Burma*. Cambridge, UK: Cambridge University Press. Retrieved July 12, 2021 (doi: /10.1017/CBO9781107051034).

Michalon, Martin, Yanni Gunnell, Jérôme Lejot, François Mialhe and Toe Aung. 2019. "Accelerated Degradation of Lake Inle (Myanmar): A Baseline Study for Environmentalists and Developers". *Land Degradation and Development* 30(8): 928-941. doi: 10.1002/ldr.3279

Ministry of Health, Department of Traditional Medicine. n.d. "Medicinal Plants of Myanmar". Retrieved July 13, 2021 (https://www.dtm.gov.mm/sites/default/files/MedicinalplantsofMyanmar-Vol(1).pdf).

Tun, Win Than. 2002. 'Myanmar Buddhism of the Pagan Period (AD 1000-1300)'. PhD dissertation, Southeast Asian Studies Programme, National University of Singapore. Retrieved from ScholarBank@NUS, 10635/13540.

Chapter 5: Indonesia

Arnold, Carrie. 2012. 'There's Something Special About Islands'. *Science*, August 7. Retrieved July 12, 2021 (https://www.sciencemag.org/news/2012/08/theres-something-special-about-islands).

Bird, Michael. 2005. "Figure 4" in [Bird, Michael, David Taylor and Chris Hunt. 2005. "Palaeoenvironments of Insular Southeast Asia During the Last Glacial Period: A Savannah Corridor to Sundaland?" *Quaternary Science Reviews* 24: 2228-2242. doi: 10.1016/j.quascirev.2005.04.004.]

Encyclopedia Britannica. 2017. 'Rafflesiaceae'. Retrieved July 12, 2020 (https://www.britannica.com/plant/Rafflesiaceae#ref268663).

Encyclopedia Britannica. 2019. 'Pitcher Plant'. Retrieved July 12, 2021 (https://www.britannica.com/plant/pitcher-plant).

Encyclopedia Britannica. n.d. 'History of Borneo'. Retrieved July 12, 2021 (https://www.britannica.com/place/Borneo-island-Pacific-Ocean/History).

Losos, Jonathan B. 2009. 'Adaptation and Diversification on Islands'. *Nature* 457(7231): 830-836. doi: 10.1038/nature07893.

Molina, Jeanmarie, Khaled M. Hazzouri, Daniel Nickrent, Matthew Geisler, Rachel S. Meyer, Melissa M. Pentony, Jonathan M. Flowers, Pieter Pelser, Julie Barcelona, Samuel Alan Inovejas, Iris Uy, Wei Yuan, Olivia Wilkins, Claire-Iphanise Michel, Selina Locklear, Gisela P. Concepcion and Michel D. Purugganan. 2014. 'Possible Loss of the Chloroplast Genome in the Parasitic Flowering Plant Rafflesia Lagascae (Rafflesiaceae)'. *Molecular Biology and Evolution* 31(4): 793-803. doi: 10.1093/molbev/msu051.

Mursidawati, Sofi, Ngatari, Irawati, Sarah Cardinal and Richa Kusumawati. 2021. '*Ex Situ* Conservation of *Rafflesia Patma* Blume (Rafflesiaceae): An Endangered Emblematic Parasitic Species from Indonesia'. *Sibbaldia: The International Journal of Botanic Garden Horticulture* 13. Retrieved July 12, 2021 (https://journals.rbge.org.uk/rbgesib/article/view/77/59).

Safran, Rebecca J. and Patrik Nosil. 2012. 'Speciation: The Origin of New Species'. *Scitable by Nature Education*. Retrieved July 12, 2021 (https://www.nature.com/scitable/knowledge/library/speciation-the-origin-of-new-species-26230527/).

Sen Nag, Oishimaya. 2017. 'Animals of Borneo'. *World Atlas*. Retrieved July 12, 2021 (https://www.worldatlas.com/articles/animals-of-borneo.html).

Sreekumari, M. T. 2001. 'Dormancy and Viability of Amorphophallus Seeds'. *Tropical Agriculture* 78(1). Retrieved July 12, 2021 (https://journals.sta.uwi.edu/ojs/index.php/ta/article/view/1404).

World Wildlife Fund. n.d. "Borneo Forests". Retrieved July 13, 2021 (https://wwf.panda.org/discover/knowledge_hub/where_we_work/borneo_forests/about_borneo_forests/borneo_animals/borneo_plants/).

World Wildlife Fund. n.d. "Dipterocarp Forests". Retrieved July 13, 2021 (https://wwf.panda.org/discover/knowledge_hub/where_we_work/borneo_forests/about_borneo_forests/ecosystems/lowland_dipterocarp/).

Chapter 6: Israel

Ashkenasi, Eli, Yoav Avni and Yona Chen. 2019. "The Vitality of Fruit Trees in Ancient Bedouin Orchards in the Arid Negev Highlands (Israel): Implications of Climatic Change and Environmental Stability". *Quaternary International* 545: 73-86. doi: 10.1016/j.quaint.2019.09.039.

Fragman-Sapir, Ori. 2016. *Daffodil, Snowdrop and Tulip Yearbook 2016*. London, UK: Royal Horticultural Society. Retrieved July 13, 2021 (https://www.botanic.co.il/wp-content/uploads/2017/12/Tulip_conservation_2016_short.pdf).

Fragman-Sapir, Ori. 2017. "Conservation in the Middle East: Local and International Collaborations". *Annals of Missouri Botanic Garden* 102(2): 319-323. doi: 10.3417/D-16-00013A.

Fragman-Sapir, Ori. n.d. "The Olive Alone". *Jerusalem Botanic Gardens*. Retrieved July 13, 2021 (https://www.botanic.co.il/wp-content/uploads/2017/09/Olea_2014_Quail_Tracks_26-1-Jan-2015-1.pdf).

Frankenberg, Eliezer. 2016. *Israel's Fifth National Report to the United Nations Convention on Biological Diversity*. Jerusalem, Israel: Ministry of Environmental Protection. Retrieved July 13, 2021 (https://www.cbd.int/doc/world/il/il-nr-05-en.pdf).

Joel, Daniel M. and Hanan Eizenberg. 2002. "Three Orobanche Species Newly Found on Crops in Israel". *Phytoparasitica* 30(2): 187-190. doi:10.1007/BF02979701.

Salehi, M., S. H. Esmailzadeh, S. Ahmadi Ghasem Kheyli, A. Fazeltabar Malekshah and M. Zaroudi. 2019. "*Cistanche Tubulosa* Could be Considered as Medicinal Plant in Halophytes Farming". Pp. 293-233 in *Halophytes: Identification, Characterization and Uses*, edited by R. Tucker. New York: Nova Science Publishers.

Retrieved July 12, 2021 (https://www.researchgate.net/publication/332711481_CISTANCHE_TUBLULOSA_COULD_BE_CONSIDERED_AS_MEDICINAL_PLANT_IN_HALOPHYTES_FARMING_Complimentary_Contributor_Copy).

Science Direct. n.d. "Geophytes". Retrieved July 13, 2021 (https://www.sciencedirect.com/topics/agricultural-and-biological-sciences/geophytes).

The Jerusalem Botanical Gardens. n.d. "About the Garden". Retrieved July 12, 2021 (https://www.botanic.co.il/en/about-the-garden/).

Chapter 7: Tanzania

Bussmann, Rainer W., Genevieve G. Gilbreath, John Solio, Manja Lutura, Rampac Lutuluo, Kimaren Kunguru, Nick Wood and Simon G. Mathenge. 2006. "Plant Use of the Maasai of Sekenani Valley, Maasai Mara, Kenya". *Journal of Ethnobiology and Ethnomedicine* 2(22). doi: 10.1186/1746-4269-2-22.

Hunter, Anna. 2017. "The Hadza Diet: How Eating Like a Hunter-Gatherer Benefits Your Gut". *Get the Gloss*, October 26. Retrieved July 12, 2020 (https://www.getthegloss.com/news/the-hazda-diet-how-eating-like-a-hunter-gatherer-benefits-your-gut).

Jigam, Ali A., Usman T. Abdulrazaq, Halima A. Mahmud and Falilat O. Tijani. "Efficacy of *Thonningia Sanguinea* Vahl. (Balanophoraceae) Root Extract Against *Plasmodium Berghei, Plasmodium Chabaudi*, Inflammation and Nociception in Mice". *Journal of Applied Pharmaceutical Science* 2(1). Retrieved July 12, 2021 (https://www.japsonline.com/admin/php/uploads/340_pdf.pdf).

Marlowe, Frank W. and Julia C. Berbesque. 2009. "Tubers as Fallback Foods and Their Impact on Hadza Hunter-Gatherers. *American Journal of Physical Anthropology* 140(4): 751-758. doi: 10.1002/ajpa.21040.

Saini, Sangita, Harmeet Kaur, Bharat Verma and Shailendra Kumar Singh. 2008. "Kigelia Africana (Lam.) Benth: An Overview". *Natural Product Radiance* 8(2). Retrieved July 12, 2021 (https://www.researchgate.net/publication/242739648_Kigelia_africana_Lam_Benth_-_An_overview).

Chapter 8: India

Chaudhuri, Panarbasu, Subarna Bhattacharyya and Alok Chandra Samal. 2016. "Living Root Bridge: A Potential No Cost Eco-technology for Mitigating Rural Communication Problems". *International Journal of Experimental Research and Review* 5. Retrieved July 13, 2020 (http://www.academia.edu/28173353/Living_Root_Bridge_A_potential_no_cost_eco-technology_for_mitigating_rural_communication_problems).

Garden Visit. n.d. "Mahtab Bagh (Moonlight Garden)". Retrieved July 12, 2021 (https://www.gardenvisit.com/gardens/mahtab_bagh-moonlight_garden).

Middleton, Wilfred, Amin Habbi, Sanjeev Shankar and Ferdinand Ludwig. 2020. "Characterizing Regenerative Aspects of Living Root Bridges". *Sustainability* 12(8). Retrieved July 13, 2021 (https://www.researchgate.net/publication/340785335_Characterizing_Regenerative_Aspects_of_Living_Root_Bridges).

Sangma, Bebeto R. and Magdalene Peter. 2021. "Living Root Bridges of Meghalaya". *Malaya Journal of Matematik* S(2). Retrieved 13 July, 2020 (https://www.malayajournal.org/articles/MJM0S200863.pdf).

Shah, Bipin. n.d. "Taj Mahal: A 'True Story' – Was it a Love Memorial or Mausoleum?" *Academia*. Retrieved July 13, 2021 (https://www.academia.edu/6641399/Taj_Mahal_A_True_Story_Was_It_a_Love_Memorial_or_Mausoleum).

Sinha, Amita. 2009. "Views of the Taj: Figure in the Landscape". *Landscape Journal* 28(2): 198-217. doi: 10.3368/lj.28.2.198.

Chapter 9: Nepal

Botanics Stories. 2017. "*Rhododendron Arboreum*: Nepal's National Flower". Retrieved July 13, 2021 (https://stories.rbge.org.uk/archives/25271).

Cultural Atlas. n.d. "Nepalese Culture: Religion". Retrieved July 13, 2021 (https://culturalatlas.sbs.com.au/nepalese-culture/nepalese-culture-religion#nepalese-culture-religion).

Duprez, Wilko. 2016. "Terracing: A Double-Edged Solution for Farming Difficult Landscapes". *Solutions*, September 16. Retrieved July 13, 2020 (https://thesolutionsjournal.com/2016/09/16/terracing-double-edged-solution-farming-difficult-landscapes/).

Encyclopedia Britannica. 2021. "Mount Everest". Retrieved July 13, 2021 (https://www.britannica.com/place/Mount-Everest).

Faiia, Scott. 2010. "Nepal's Magnificent Rhododendron". *ECS Nepal*, June. Retrieved July 13, 2021 (http://ecs.com.np/features/nepals-magnificent-rhododendron).

J. B. Abington. 1992. *Sustainable Livestock Production in the Mountain Agro-Ecosystem of Nepal*. FAO Animal Production and Health Paper 105. Rome, Italy: Food and Agriculture Organization of the United Nations. Retrieved 13 July, 2021 (http://www.fao.org/3/t0706e/T0706E00.htm#TOC).

Jansen, Suze A., Iris Kleerekooper, Zonne L. M. Hofman, Isabelle F. P. M. Kappen, Anna Stary-Weinzinger and Marcel A. G. van der Heyden. "Grayanotoxin Poisoning: 'Mad Honey Disease' and Beyond". *Cardiovascular Toxicology* 12(3): 208-215. doi: 10.1007/s12012-012-9162-2

Khadka, Luna. 2013. "Age Structure and Regeneration of *Rhododendron Arboreum* Sm. Along an Altitudinal Gradient of Manaslu Conservation Area, Nepal Himalaya". Master's thesis, Central Department of Environmental Science, Tribhuvan University.

Knörzer, Karl-Heinz. 2000. "3000 Years of Agriculture in a Valley of the High Himalayas". *Vegetation History and Archaeobotany* 9(4): 219-222. doi: 10.1007/BF01294636.

Milner Gardens and Woodland. n.d. "The Rhododendrons of Milner Gardens and Woodland". Retrieved July 13, 2021 (https://milnergardens.viu.ca/sites/default/files/milnergardensandwoodland-rhododendronbooklet.pdf).

Ollerton, Jeff, Narayan P. Kohu, Sanu R. Maharjan, Bijay Bashyal. 2019. "Interactions Between Birds and Flowers of *Rhododendron* spp., and their Implications for Mountain Communities in Nepal". *Plants People Planet* (19 November, 2019). Retrieved 13 July, 2020 (https://nph.onlinelibrary.wiley.com/doi/epdf/10.1002/ppp3.10091).

Pandit, Karun and Mohan K. Balla. 2004. "Indigenous Knowledge of Terrace Management in Paundi Khola Watershed, Lamjung District, Nepal". *Himalayan Journal of Sciences* 2(3). Retrieved July 13, 2021 (https://www.researchgate.net/publication/280684438_Indigenous_knowledge_of_terrace_management_in_Paundi_Khola_watershed_Lamjung_district_Nepal).

Thapa, Anju. n.d. "Pagoda". *Pagoda Architecture in Kathmandu*. Retrieved July 13, 2021 (https://www.webpages.uidaho.edu/arch499/nonwest/nepal/Pagoda.htm).

Waelti, Corinne and Dorothee Spuhler. n.d. "Bunds". *Sustainable Sanitation and Water Management Toolbox*. Retrieved July 13, 2021 (https://sswm.info/sswm-university-course/module-4-sustainable-water-supply/further-resources-water-sources-hardware/bunds).

Wiggins, Steve and Anita Ghimire. 2016. *Nepal Terrace Farmers and SAKs*. Canadian International Food Security Research Fund. Ottowa, Canada: IDRC. Retrieved July 13, 2021 (https://idl-bnc-idrc.dspacedirect.org/bitstream/handle/10625/57266/IDL-57266.pdf?sequence=2&isAllowed=y).

Chapter 10: Solomon Islands

Davenport, William. 1962. "Red-Feather Money". *Scientific American*, March. Retrieved July 12, 2021 (https://www.scientificamerican.com/article/red-feather-money/).

Lavery, Tyrone, Patrick Pikacha and Diana Fisher. 2016. "Solomon Islands Forest Life: Information on Biology and Management of Forest Resources". *Critical Ecosystem Partnership Fund*. Retrieved July 13, 2021 (https://espace.library.uq.edu.au/view/UQ:387049/UQ387049_OA_quick_download.pdf).

Makky, Khadijah I. and Audra A. Kramer. 2016. "Dark Skin, Blond Hair: Surprise in the Solomon Islands". *National Center for Case Study Teaching in Science*. Retrieved July 13, 2021 (https://sciencecases.lib.buffalo.edu/files/dark_skin_blond.pdf).

Ministry of Agriculture and Fisheries. 1996. *Solomon Islands: Country Report*. FAO International Technical Conference on Plant Genetic Resources. Rome, Italy: Food and Agriculture Organization of the United Nations. Retrieved 13 July, 2021 (http://www.fao.org/fileadmin/templates/agphome/documents/PGR/SoW1/asia/SOLOMONI.pdf).

Mollick, A. S., H. Shimoji, Tetsuo Denda and Masatsugu Yokota. 2011. "Croton Codiaeum Variegatum (L.) Blume Cultivars Characterized by Leaf Phenotypic Parameters". *Scientifica Horticulturae* 132(1): 71-79. doi: 10.1016/j.scienta.2011.09.038.

O'Brien, Patricia, J. 1972. "The Sweet Potato: Its Origin and Dispersal". *American Anthropologist* 74(3): 342-365. doi: 10.1525/aa.1972.74.3.02a00070.

Ross, Harold M. 1977. "The Sweet Potato in the South-Eastern Solomons". *The Journal of the Polynesian Society* 86(4). Retrieved July 13, 2021 (https://www.jstor.org/stable/20705298).

Rowe, Derrick, J. 2014. "Epiphytic Myrmecophytes of Southern Asia and the Southwest Pacific". *Xerophilia* special issue no. 3 (January 2014). Retrieved July 12, 2021 (https://xerophilia.ro/wp-content/uploads/2014/02/epiphytic-myrmecophytes-revised.pdf).

Sachter-Smith, Gabriel. 2011. "Bananas of the Solomon Islands". Retrieved July 13, 2021 (http://www.musalit.org/viewPdf.php?file=IN140215.pdf&id=15133).

Sheppard, Peter J. and Richard Walter. 2006. "A Revised Model of Solomon Islands Culture History". *Journal of Polynesian Society* 115. Retrieved July 13, 2021 (https://www.researchgate.net/publication/251992785_A_Revised_Model_of_Solomon_Islands_Culture_History).

Sheppard, Peter J., Richard Walter and Takuya Nagaoka. 2000. "The Archaeology of Head-Hunting in Roviana Lagoon, New Georgia, Solomon Islands". *The Journal of the Polynesian Society* 109(1). Retrieved July 12, 2021 (https://www.researchgate.net/publication/286920738_The_archaeology_of_head-hunting_in_Roviana_Lagoon_New_Georgia_Solomon_Islands).

Chapter 11: Bhutan

A Way to Bhutan Tours and Travels. 2020. "Architecture of Bhutan". Retrieved July 13, 2021 (https://waytobhutan.com/architecture-of-bhutan/).

Bhattacharya, Nilanjan. n.d. "Giant Statue of Buddha in Meditation in Front of a Pagoda in Bhutan". Image (JPEG). Retrieved July 13, 2021 (https://www.dreamstime.com/stock-photo-buddha-meditation-giant-statue-front-pagoda-bhutan-image78867648).

Druk Metho. n.d. "Druk Metho: Blossoms of Bhutan". Retrieved July 13, 2021 (https://drukmetho.com/).

Dworecka-Kaszak, Bożena. 2014. "Cordyceps Fungi as Natural Killers, New Hopes for Medicine and Biological Control Factors". *Annals of Parasitology* 60(3). Retrieved July 13, 2021 (https://pubmed.ncbi.nlm.nih.gov/25281812/).

Explore Himalayas. n.d. "National Flower of Bhutan". Retrieved July 13, 2021 (http://www.himalaya2000.com/bhutan/national-symbols/national-flower.html).

Greek City Times. 2020. "The Oldest Olive Tree in the World: Elia Vouvon". Retrieved July 13, 2021 (https://greekcitytimes.com/2020/09/15/the-oldest-olive-tree-in-the-world-elia-vouvon/).

Heronswood. 2017. "A Gross Happiness of Blue". Retrieved July 13, 2021 (https://heronswoodgarden.org/a-gross-happiness-of-blue/).

Lo, Hui-Chen, Chienyan Hsieh, Fang-Yi-Lin and Tai-Hao Hsu. 2013. "A Systematic Review of the Mysterious Caterpillar Fungus *Ophiocordyceps Sinensis* in Dong-ChongXiaCao and Related Bioactive Ingredients". *Journal of Traditional and Complementary Medicine* 3(1): 16-32. doi: 10.4103/2225-4110.106538

Sung, Gi-Ho, Nigel L. Hywel-Jones, Jae-Mo Sung, J. Jennifer Luangsa-ard, Bhushan Shrestha and Joseph W. Spatafora. 2007. "Phylogenetic Classification of *Cordyceps* and the Clavicipitaceous Fungi". *Studies in Mycology* 57: 5-59. doi: 10.3114/sim.2007.57.01

The Gymnosperm Database. n.d. "Cupressus Torulosa". Retrieved July 13, 2021 (https://www.conifers.org/cu/Cupressus_torulosa.php).

The Gymnosperm Database. n.d. "Pinus Bhutanica". Retrieved July 13, 2021 (https://www.conifers.org/pi/Pinus_bhutanica.php).

van de Walle, Gavin. 2018. "6 Benefits of Cordyceps, All Backed by Science". *Healthline*. Retrieved July 13, 2021 (https://www.healthline.com/nutrition/cordyceps-benefits).

Wangdi, Tempa. 2017. "National Flower, Blue Poppy is a New Species". *Kuensel*. Retrieved July 13, 2021 (https://kuenselonline.com/national-flower-blue-poppy-is-a-new-species/).

Wu, Hua, Zhong-Chen Rao, Li Cao, Patrick De Clercq and Ri-Chou Han. 2020. "Infection of *Ophiocordyceps Sinensis* Fungus Causes Dramatic Changes in the Microbiota of Its *Thitarodes* Host. *Frontiers in Microbiology* (December 3, 2020). doi: 10.3389/fmicb.2020.577268.

Chapter 12: Singapore

Gardens by the Bay. 2018. "Information Guide". Retrieved July 13, 2021 (https://www.gardensbythebay.com.sg/content/dam/gbb/plan-your-visit/info-guide/information-guide-english-2018.pdf).

Ingenia. 2014. "Singapore's Supertrees". Retrieved July 13, 2021 (http://www.solaripedia.com/files/1190.pdf).

Zappi, Daniela C. 2013. *Guides to Gardens by the Bay: Heritage Garden Plants and Recipes.* Singapore: NUS Museum. Retrieved 13 July, 2021 (https://www.researchgate.net/publication/259826994_Guides_to_Gardens_by_the_Bay_Heritage_Garden_Plants_and_Recipes).

Zappi, Daniela C. 2014. *Water Sustainability System at Gardens by the Bay*. Singapore: NUS Museum. Retrieved July 13, 2021 (https://www.researchgate.net/publication/259828061_Water_Sustainability_System_at_Gardens_by_the_Bay).

Glossary of Terms

Aesthetic - concerned with beauty or the appreciation of beauty

Alleviate - make suffering, deficiency or a problem less severe

Altitude - the height of an object or point in relation to sea level or ground level

Ambience - the character and atmosphere of a place

Amenity horticulture - cultivation and care of private and municipal grounds and open spaces, especially of gardens, parks, and other areas used for pleasure and recreation

Anoxia - an absence of oxygen

Anthropologist - an expert in the study of human societies and cultures and their development

Aphrodisiac - a food, drink, or drug that stimulates sexual desire

Aqueducts - an artificial channel for conveying water, typically in the form of a bridge across a valley or other gap

Aquifer - a body of permeable rock which can contain or transmit groundwater

Arable - describes land used or suitable for growing crops

Archipelago - a group of islands

Arduous - involving or requiring strenuous effort; difficult and tiring

Arterial - denoting an important route in a system of roads, railroad lines, or rivers

Atolls - a ring-shaped reef, island, or chain of islands formed of coral

Authenticity - the quality of being of undisputed origin

Ayurvedic medicine - a system of healing that originated in ancient India, ayur being Sanskrit for life and veda meaning knowledge

Bazaar - a market in a Middle Eastern country

Bereft - deprived of or lacking something

Bioluminescent - having a biochemical emission of light by living organisms such as fireflies and deep-sea fishes

Biophilic - having an attraction to all that is alive and vital

Charismatic - exercising a compelling charm which inspires devotion in others

Cistern - an underground reservoir for rainwater

Conservatory - a room with a glass roof and walls

Contentious - causing or likely to cause an argument; controversial

Convergent evolution - the independent evolution of similar features in species of different periods or epochs in time

Degradation - changing to a lower state or level

Delta - a triangular tract of sediment deposited at the mouth of a river, typically where it diverges into several outlets

Desert - a dry, barren area of land, especially one covered with sand, that is characteristically desolate, waterless, and without vegetation

Diffusion - the spreading of something more widely

Diversification - the action of diversifying something or the fact of becoming more diverse

Dysentery - infection of the intestines resulting in severe diarrhea

Eclectic - deriving ideas, style, or taste from a broad and diverse range of sources

El Niño Southern Oscillation - the oscillation between the El Niño climate phase and the La Niña phase, usually over several years

Encroachment - intrusion on a person's territory, rights, etc.

Endemic - a plant or animal which is native and restricted to a certain place

Enthral - capture the fascinated attention of

Entomopathogenic - lethally parasitic upon insects

Ephemerals - plants which last or exist for a very short time

Epicentre - the central point of something

Epiphyte - a plant that grows on another plant but is not parasitic

Epiphytic - adjectival form of epiphyte

Ethnobotanical - of the scientific study of the traditional knowledge and customs of a people concerning plants and their medical, religious, and other uses

Evanescent - soon passing out of sight, memory, or existence; quickly fading or disappearing

Exploitation - the action of making use of and benefiting from resources

Fallow - farmland ploughed and harrowed but left unsown for a period in order to restore its fertility

Fissures - a long, narrow opening or line of breakage made by cracking or splitting, especially in rock or earth

Flamboyant - noticeable because brightly coloured, highly patterned, or unusual in style

Floriculture - the cultivation of flowers

Fortunate - materially well-off; prosperous

Gargantuan - enormous

Genera - the usual major subdivision of a biological family or subfamily in the classification of organisms

Genomic sequencing - method of detecting genetic information of organisms

Geophytes - plants typically with underground storage organs, where the plants hold energy and water

Germination - the development of a plant from a seed or spore after a period of dormancy

Governance - the action or manner of governing

Grafting - horticultural technique whereby tissues of plants are joined so as to continue their growth together

Grand caravan - a group of people, especially traders or pilgrims, traveling together

Haustoria - a slender projection from the root of a parasitic plant which enables the parasite to penetrate the tissues of its host and absorb its nutrients

Herptiles – amphibians and reptiles

Hydraulics - the branch of science and technology concerned with the conveyance of liquids through pipes and channels

Hydrophytes - plants which grow only in or on water

Indigenous - originating or occurring naturally in a particular place; native

Inflorescence - the arrangement of the flowers on a plant

Innately - as an inborn characteristic; naturally

Inosculation - a natural phenomenon in which trunks, branches or roots of two trees grow together

Intrinsically - in an essential or natural way

Islets - small islands

Lanceolate - shaped like the head of a lance; of a narrow oval shape tapering to a point at each end

Leguminous - relating to or denoting plants of the pea family (Leguminosae).

Lineages - lineal descent from an ancestor; ancestry or pedigree

Locavore - a diet consisting only or principally of locally grown or produced food

Longevity - long existence, life or service

Luminous - full of or shedding light; bright or shining, especially in the dark

Mangrove - a tidal swamp that is dominated by mangroves and associated vegetation

Mausoleum - a building, especially a large and stately one, housing a tomb or tombs

Microclimates - the climate of a very small or restricted area, especially when this differs from the climate of the surrounding area

Mitigate - make less severe, serious or painful

Monocultures - cultivations of a single crop in a given area

Monsoon - the season of heavy rain during the summer in hot Asian countries

Monsoonal - adjectival form of monsoon

Montane - of or inhabiting mountainous country

Mucilaginous - containing a polysaccharide substance that is extracted as a viscous or gelatinous solution

Mutualistic - having mutual dependence between two organisms

Naturalised - established (a plant or animal) so that it lives wild in a region where it is not indigenous/native

Naturalist - an expert in or student of natural history

Nullifying - make of no use or value

Osmotic processes - a process by which molecules of a solvent tend to pass through a semipermeable membrane from a less concentrated solution into a more concentrated one, thus equalising the concentrations on each side of the membrane

Pagodas - a Hindu or Buddhist temple or sacred building, typically a many-tiered tower

Palaeoethnobotanical - the study of fossil seeds and grains to further archaeological knowledge, particularly the domestication of cereals

Palette - range or variety of a particular property

Paradox - a seemingly absurd or self-contradictory statement or proposition that when investigated or explained may prove to be well founded or true

Parasitic - of an organism which lives on and exploits another organism

Pavilion - a decorative building used as a shelter in a park or large garden.

Pedestrian - lacking inspiration or excitement; dull

Perennial - lasting or existing for a long or apparently infinite time

Periphery - the outer limits or edge of an area or object

Permaculture - the development of agricultural ecosystems intended to be sustainable and self-sufficient

Phenols - a family of organic compounds

Phenolic - adjectival form of phenol

Physiologically - in a way that relates to the functions of living organisms and their parts

Phytogeographical - pertaining to the branch of botany that deals with the geographical distribution of plants

Pioneering - involving new ideas or methods

Plethora - a large or excessive amount of (something)

Porous - having minute spaces or holes through which liquid or air may pass

Poultice - a soft, moist mass of material, typically of plant material or flour, applied to the body to relieve soreness and inflammation and kept in place with a cloth

Precarious - dependent on chance; uncertain

Prodigious - remarkably or impressively great in extent, size, or degree

Prolific - producing much fruit or foliage or many offspring

Quintessentially - used to emphasize the most perfect or typical example of a quality or class

Resins - sticky organic substances, insoluble in water, exuded by some trees and other plants

Reverberates - appears to vibrate or be disturbed because of a loud noise

Riparian - relating to wetlands adjacent to rivers and streams

Sanctity - the state or quality of being holy, sacred, or saintly

Savannah - a grassy plain in tropical and subtropical regions, with few trees

Seclusion - the state of being private and away from other people

Sedentary - inhabiting the same locality throughout life; not migratory or nomadic.

Sedimentary - (of rock) that has formed from sediment deposited by water or air

Serotonin - a compound present in blood platelets and serum, which constricts the blood vessels and acts as a neurotransmitter

Shangri-La - a place regarded as an earthly paradise, especially when involving a retreat from the pressures of modern civilization

Speciation - the formation of new and distinct species in the course of evolution

Steppe - a large area of flat unforested grassland

Stimulus - a thing or event that evokes a specific functional reaction in an organ or tissue

Subsistence - denoting or relating to production at a level sufficient only for one's own use or consumption, without any surplus for trade

Supplementary - completing or enhancing something

Sustainably - in a way that avoids the depletion of natural resources in order to maintain an ecological balance

Swales - a low or hollow place, especially a marshy depression between ridges.

Swathe - a broad strip or area of something

Sylphid - a young, imaginary spirit of the air

Synthesised - made something by combining different things

Taxonomical - concerned with the classification of things, especially organisms

Tenacious - persisting in existence; not easily dispelled

Terrestrial - of, on or relating to the earth

Topiary - the art or practice of clipping shrubs or trees into ornamental shapes

Tubers - a much thickened underground part of a stem, e.g. in the potato, serving as a food reserve and bearing buds from which new plants arise

Uncatalogued - not systematically listed as a collection

Understorey - a layer of vegetation beneath the main canopy of a forest

Unisexual - (of a flower) having either stamens or pistils but not both

Usurped - had a position of power or importance taken illegally or by force

Venturesome - willing to take risks or embark on difficult or unusual courses of action

Vertiginous - causing vertigo, especially by being extremely high or steep

Viticulture - the cultivation of grapevines.

Vying - competing eagerly with someone or something in order to do or achieve something

Xerophyte - a plant which needs very little water

Xerophytic - adjectival form of xerophyte

Image Attributions With Thanks

Cover: Credit Gardens by the Bay

Page 1: Bengal tiger prowling the Sundarbans - credit Soumyajit Nandy

     Aerial view of the Ratargul Forest - credit Kazi Asadullah Al Emran

Page 4: Woman weaving shitol pati - credit Faizul Latif Chowdhury

Page 5: *Millettia pinnata* - credit Vinayaraj

Page 6: *Crataeva magna* - credit Vinayaraj

Page 12: Wadi Rum at sunset - credit Chris White

Page 14: *Cupressus sempervirens* and carved stone dwelling - credit Chris White

Page 16: *Sternbergia clusiana* and leaves of *Drimia aphylla* - credit Chris White

Page 20: Swales dry out quickly without shade from larger plants - credit Adeeb Atwan

Page 23: *Orchis mascula* one of the orchids used in salep - credit xulescu_g

     Cup of Turkish salep - credit E4024

Page 24: Fairy chimneys and farming in Cappadocia - credit Benh Lieu Song

Pages 29 to 32: All images - credit Relais and Chateaux Museum Hotel

Page 33: Apricots drying in the Cappadocian sun -credit Bjørn Christian Tørrissen

Page 48: Winged fruit of the Dipterocarpaceae family - credit Bernard Dupont

Page 52: *Rafflesia patma* images - credit Sofi Mursidawati

Page 54: Tetrasigma vine parasitised by *Rafflesia patma* being grafted on to a new host

     Rafflesia patma being packed for the International Horticulture Goyang

     - credits Sofi Mursidawati

Pages 55 to 57: All images - credit Matt Coulter

Page 58: A titan arum flowering at the New York Botanic Gardens - credit Rhododendrites

Page 69: Lotuses in bloom on Jerusalem Botanic Gardens' feature lake - credit Tom Amit

Page 66: View inside the Jerusalem Botanic Gardens' tropical conservatory - credit Tom Amit

Page 67: The conservatory nearing the end of its recent construction - credit Tom Amit

Page 102: Flowers of the tree rhododendron (*Rhododendron arboreum*) - credit Biplab Anand

Page 107: Makira produces an extensive variety of bananas - credit Yvonne Green

     Paper mulberry (Broussonetia papyrifera) - credit Zeynel Cebeci

     Photo of Kaipua Angikitasi Paa'ungahenua

     Member of Kaumaakonga- A Traditional/ Contemporary band from Mungiki ma Mungava

     Photographer: Nikki Michail (Sustainable Dreaming)

Page 109: Bioluminescent fungi (*Mycena chlorophos*) - credit Chris White

Page 110: Ant plant (*Myrmecodia tuberosa* 'Salomonensis') - credit Brendan Cleaver

Page 115: Red feather money of Makira - credit Hiart

Page 119: Honiara flower market - credit Yvonne Green

Page 130: Bhutan's national flower (*Meconopsis gakyidiana*) credit - Toshio Yoshida, Rinchen Yangzom and Long, David.

Page 133 to 140: All images - credit Gardens by the Bay

Page 142: 'Blossom Beats' display within the Flower Dome - credit Gardens by the Bay

Pages 143 and 144: Both images - credit Gardens by the Bay

www.ingramcontent.com/pod-product-compliance
Lightning Source LLC
Chambersburg PA
CBHW061135030426

42334CB00003B/49